"*The Gambling Disorder Treatment Handbook* by Jody Bechtold and Alyssa Wilson is the most comprehensive, current guide for the treatment of gambling disorder I have encountered. It provides a solid, evidence-informed rationale for a broad range of treatment approaches while also addressing 'real-life' clinical applications. The authors, using their significant clinical experience, also address under-researched topics that are critical to the treatment of gambling disorder, such as financial management, restitution, money protection planning, and coping with legal issues. This book is a must-have for any clinician working with clients and their families struggling with gambling disorder."

—*Lori Rugle, PhD, ICGC-II/BACC, Program Director,*
Center of Excellence on Problem Gambling

"New to treating gambling disorders? Struggling to translate theory/research? Well, Bechtold and Wilson provide an updated, clear, concise, practical, and evidence-based treatment guide. Current trends, gambling subtypes, holistic emphasis, case illustrations, and models of intervention–application connect the dots! This is a must-read treatment roadmap for every addiction professional."

—*Deborah G. Haskins, Ph.D., LCPC, ACS, MAC, ICGC-II, CCGSO,*
BACC, Owner/Chief Clinical Consultant—MOSAIC Consulting and
Counseling Services President, Maryland Council on Problem Gambling

"I am sure the clinicians that will utilize this book will gain the knowledge necessary to provide excellent therapeutic skills to the problem/disordered gambler. I look forward to being able to share this book with our treatment providers. The case studies will help the clinician to understand the dynamics of the problem/disordered gambler. I would recommend this book to others in this field."

—*Neva Pryor, MS, Executive Director of the Council*
on Compulsive Gambling of New Jersey

of related interest

Counselling Skills for Working with Trauma
Healing from Child Sexual Abuse, Sexual
Violence and Domestic Abuse
Christiane Sanderson
ISBN 978 1 84905 326 6
eISBN 978 0 85700 743 8

Counselling Skills for Working with Shame
Christiane Sanderson
ISBN 978 1 84905 562 8
eISBN 978 1 78450 001 6

**Drinking, Drug Use, and Addiction
in the Autism Community**
Elizabeth Kunreuther and Ann Palmer
Foreword by Tony Attwood
ISBN 978 1 78592 749 2
eISBN 978 1 78450 539 4

**Supporting People Bereaved through
a Drug- or Alcohol-Related Death**
Peter Cartwright
ISBN 978 1 78592 191 9
eISBN 978 1 78450 463 2

THE GAMBLING DISORDER TREATMENT HANDBOOK

A Guide for Mental Health Professionals

JODY BECHTOLD AND **ALYSSA WILSON**

Jessica Kingsley Publishers
London and Philadelphia

First published in Great Britain in 2021 by Jessica Kingsley Publishers
An Hachette Company

1

Copyright © Jody Bechtold and Alyssa Wilson 2021

Gambling disorder criteria on page 88 is reprinted with permission from
Diagnostic and Statistical Manual of Mental Disorders, Fifth Edition (Copyright
© 2013). American Psychiatric Association. All Rights Reserved.
Gambling disorder criteria on pages 89–90 is reproduced with permission
from *International Statistical Classification of Diseases and Related
Health Problems, 11th ed*, World Health Organization, 2019.
The Gambling Biopsychosocial-Spiritual Evaluation on pages
105–129 is modified from Ladouceur and Lachance 2007 with
permission of Oxford Publishing Limited through PLSclear.

A CIP catalogue record for this title is available from the
British Library and the Library of Congress

ISBN 978 1 78775 552 9
eISBN 978 1 78775 553 6

Printed and bound in the United States by Integrated Books International

Jessica Kingsley Publishers' policy is to use papers that are natural,
renewable and recyclable products and made from wood grown in
sustainable forests. The logging and manufacturing processes are expected
to conform to the environmental regulations of the country of origin.

Jessica Kingsley Publishers
Carmelite House
50 Victoria Embankment
London EC4Y 0DZ

www.jkp.com

This book is dedicated to all of those that have come before us, trained us, coached and mentored us, consulted with us, and ultimately walked side by side with us on this journey that intersects personal and professional. We could not have written this book if it wasn't for all the people dealing with problematic gambling who trusted us enough to help them at a very vulnerable and difficult time in their lives. We are forever grateful and humbled.

In memory of:
Joanna Franklin
James (Jim) Pappas
Jeffrey Beck

Contents

Acknowledgments

This book could not have been written without the multiple people who supported us and gave us opportunities to attend trainings, offer workshops, and conduct research about problem and disordered gambling.

Jody Bechtold wishes to thank the Council on Compulsive Gambling of Pennsylvania, as the very first supporter who created multiple opportunities to work with individuals with gambling problems. They continue to be a great partnership under the leadership of Josh Ercole. The University of Pittsburgh, School of Social Work, Continuing Education Department, under the direction of Tracy Soska, helped over 250 therapists learn about and work towards certification when Pennsylvania expanded legalized gambling in 2007. Dr. Ray Engel and Elizabeth Mulvaney, LCSW, have been such great supporters, advocates, researchers, and trainers, always looking for ways to further the field of problem gambling for professionals, individuals, and families. Joanna Frankin and Lori Rugle were my first mentors, and Lori continues to be a very important figure in my professional development. I am forever grateful for their leadership as they helped me on this wonderful journey that continues to be full of humility, gratitude, and purpose.

The National Council on Problem Gambling (NCPG) and the International Gambling Counselor Certification Board (IGCCB) have been pillars of support, guidance, and professional identity. The field of problem gambling may not be large, but it is a strong and mighty group of people that we are so proud to belong to and be a part of.

And thanks to my husband, John Bechtold, for always supporting me as a lifelong learner and being my biggest cheerleader to keep doing more.

Alyssa Wilson acknowledges the support received by Saint Louis University and the School of Social Work. The School has supported my research on gambling and graciously gave my casino replica research lab a space on campus. Thank you to the graduate students who have volunteered their time in the gambling lab, performing countless thesis and independent research projects, all aimed at understanding at-risk and problem gambling. I particularly want to thank my graduate assistant (GA), Laurel Giacone who, as my GA, has been exemplary in keeping the lab organized and running efficiently. I am very grateful for her attention to detail and assistance in curating the references and evidence base used herein.

A special thanks to my colleagues, Sarah Coffin, Heather Lewis, and Adam Hahs, who listened to various lectures and symposiums, edited manuscripts on my work related to problem gambling, and provided invaluable feedback. Noelle Fearn, thank you for your unwavering support, as a friend and colleague.

I am also grateful for the Salvation Army addiction treatment center in St. Louis, Missouri, and to Captain Adam Moore and Lamara Dickerson for their openness and willingness to allow me and my graduate student research team the space to work with their clients. I am thankful for all the clients we were fortunate to work with over the years, who allowed us to share in their journey towards sobriety.

Finally, thank you to my family, and husband, who continues to teach me about resiliency, strength, and finding my voice.

Preface

We are living in a time where legalized gambling is increasing globally, more than ever before. We are also seeing new forms of gambling, through online and other virtual platforms and media. With this rise in accessibility, people across the world are now given access to gamble 24/7, 365 days a year. In our respective practices, we too have seen a rise in individuals impacted by gambling.

At the same time, there is an explosion of research targeting gambling across the lifespan. While the *Journal of Gambling Issues (JGI)* was the world's first journal dedicated to problem gambling, there is now a range of peer-reviewed journals which focus solely on gambling and gambling addiction (i.e., *Journal of Gambling Studies*; *International Gambling Studies*; *Journal of Gambling*, etc.). Further, advocacy campaigns to spread psychoeducation about problem gambling have also seen a rise in popularity, with recent public health initiatives across gambling jurisdictions.

Unfortunately, there is a lack of materials available to therapists and other mental health professionals interacting with clients who may have a gambling problem. There are good journal articles that show empirically validated outcomes for specific therapies, and there are good materials available for those associated with regional and national gambling organizations (i.e., National Council on Problem Gambling and state affiliates). While experts in the field of gambling continue to conduct research and write articles and books on this subject, there hasn't been a practical clinical handbook on disordered gambling in over ten years, written specifically for therapists. That is where our book comes in.

We, the authors, set forth to write a book about the treatment of disordered gambling that would be most useful and helpful to *mental health professionals*. We wanted to share current evidence-based theories and interventions, as well as practical strategies that have been successful in our clinical practices. As individuals, we have each dedicated our research and clinical practice to serving and treating individuals and families struggling with gambling addiction. As a writing team, we bring together researcher and therapist/clinical views and experiences. Together we wanted to write a book that was specifically designed for clinicians on the front line of disordered gambling: therapists working with individuals of any age who are suffering from a gambling problem across any gambling mode (i.e., online or brick-and-mortar), activity (i.e., casino gambling vs. sports gambling), and subtype (i.e., gamblers who play to escape stress and other "bad" aspects of their life vs. gamblers who play to get free stuff). Our expertise has not only been shaped by our own experience with gambling clients, but also through the countless workshops, conferences, and webinars we have conducted (and where we have learned from the many attendees who have shared their own experiences with us).

It is our hope not only that the current book will assist the reader to understand gambling disorder from a whole-person perspective, but that the contents of the book can easily and immediately be applied to the reader's clinical practice (i.e., working with individuals with gambling disorders). The goal is that readers will develop a thorough understanding of the biopsychosocial nature of disordered gambling, which in turn will assist them in using the treatment information in the second section of the book. Additional materials discussed in Chapter 5, for instance, are available to download from www.jkp.com/catalogue/book/9781787755529. Further, we hope this book can complement various students in training, particularly for the International Certification for Gambling Counselor (ICGC), and those working to obtain "expertise" in treatment provision for problem and disordered gambling.

CHAPTER 1: GAMBLING IS EVERYWHERE

(and it doesn't appear to be going away anytime soon)

"Gambling is a fun form of entertainment,
until it no longer is fun or entertaining."

The world around us is constantly changing at rapidly growing speeds and through advancements that continue to promote, and in some instances impede, the human condition. With the rise of the Internet, global digital Internet users now include upwards of 58% of the global population (or 4.3 billion out of 7.67 billion total population: Clements, 2019). Phones more closely resemble mini computers than they do rotary phones (or "land lines"), and no longer reflect a divide in socioeconomic status. Social interactions have been influenced by technology and the Internet, as evidenced by the social media movement that seemed to dominate the 2000s, with platforms like Facebook, Twitter, and Instagram. Such technological advancements have been propelled by the limitless features of virtual worlds that developers can create online and patrons can access whenever and wherever they are. With the burgeoning advancements in technology, combined with cultural emphasis towards virtual and online forms of entertainment, accessibility to anything and everything, including gambling venues and betting shops, exists across the globe.

Gambling, or games of chance, has a long history across cultures and continents, both in terms of social support for and discontent with gambling activities. Humans have a long historical connection with gambling, as evidenced by early forms of games of chance found in Mesopotamia and China, some dating as far back as the Paleolithic (or "stone age") period (Schwartz, 2013). In today's globally connected society, legal and illegal forms of gambling activities abound.

While each country and legal jurisdiction has its own unique and idiosyncratic policies and laws on legal and illegal forms of gambling, most jurisdictions all agree on what gambling entails: a game of chance or skill (or a combination of both) that involves wagering something of value (usually money) in the hopes of winning a prize or something of greater value (usually larger sums of money). Under this definition, any form of gambling in today's world can be accessible not only through brick-and-mortar establishments, but on any electronic device that can access the Internet. Similarly, gambling is no longer something that a person has to go anywhere to do; they can access some form of it at home, at work, in their car, or wherever they may find themselves. Access has never been easier.

While it is clear that forms of gambling are here to stay in most corners of the world (with parts of the Middle East, Africa, and Asia still restricting all forms of gambling), the recent surge in technology advancements and electronic gaming innovation has led to developments of new markets and avenues for gamblers to place bets. To this end, it is imperative for those in the helping professions (i.e., therapists) to stay up to date with developments as they become available. The purpose of the current chapter is to present an initial overview of the state of gambling across the globe, as it relates to newly established and disseminated aspects of gaming types (i.e., online, sports betting, etc.).

Global Gambling Market

Worldwide, games of chance range from the more traditional casino games (including slot machines, pokies, or similar video gaming machines (VGMs);

table games like blackjack, poker, roulette, craps; keno; baccarat) and pari-mutuel betting shops (including horse racing, greyhound/dog racing), to lottery, scratch-offs, and sports betting (see also American Gaming Association, 2019b). In Western countries like Canada, the United Kingdom, and Australia, casino, lottery, and sports betting have been legal for decades or more. In the United States, 48 of the 50 states have some form of legalized gambling, with Hawaii and Utah as states that prohibit all forms of gambling (American Gaming Association, 2019b; National Council on Problem Gambling, 2019). Similarly, with the 2017 Supreme Court ruling to lift restrictions on sports betting, the United States has seen up to 21 states with legalized sports betting, with active legislation on dockets in 18 states at the time of this writing (American Gaming Association, 2019a).

In 2019, casino games were the highest grossing form of gambling with an estimated $41 billion in the United States (American Gaming Association, 2019b), and an estimated £14.4 billion in revenue between April 2018 and May 2019 in the United Kingdom (Gambling Commission, 2019). Total gambling expenditure in Australia in 2017–2018 increased by 5% from the previous year, and was estimated at $24.887 billion (Queensland Government Statistician's Office, 2019). The per adult gambling expenditure, which in 2018 was reported to be more than double that in the United States (Baidawi, 2018), also increased in 2017–2018 by 3.3% to $1,292.25 per adult (Queensland Government Statistician's Office, 2019).

Socio-cultural acceptance towards gambling is also on the rise, given the variety of new and novel ways people access forms of gambling. In addition to the brick-and-mortar gambling establishments commonly considered "traditional" such as casinos, pokie bars, pachinko bars, racetracks, etc., gambling venues are beginning to pop up in non-traditional locations across the world. For instance, in the United States, video gaming machines (VGM) are commonplace in corners of gas stations in some states (e.g., Illinois, Missouri, Pennsylvania, to name just a few), while lottery kiosks can be found in airports and other public spaces like grocery stores or restaurants. In other countries, lottery tickets are easily found and purchased in local markets (e.g., Mauritius lottery practices in 2019), while other jurisdictions allow patrons to place bets on their phones for the local pari-mutuel horse races. Furthermore, regardless of geographical jurisdiction, even aspects of popular video games include features of gambling, including wagering actual money or game money on slots or other casino games (e.g., casino sub-game within Grand Theft Auto®), and loot boxes (i.e., paying real money to access a random prize within video games) are becoming more prevalent.

Long gone are the days when people had to make a specific effort to gamble, when people had to literally go to the casino or to the racetrack, when the gambling activity had an end, a closing time. In 2020, the world is a very different place, and gambling is *everywhere*. Gambling as a culturally acceptable pastime is entrenched in the fabric of the modern, day-to-day world (with a few exceptions including online and Internet gambling restrictions in Southeast Asian nations and some Middle Eastern nations). Emerging trends in the global gambling industry will be explored in the next section, to highlight and underscore the trends in gambling expansion related to alternative forms of gambling and the corresponding trends in public policy and attitudes towards responsible gambling and similar industry standards. New and emerging forms of gambling that are possible through online or Internet platforms include sports betting and eSports, forms of social gaming (including Candy Crush, etc.), as well as enhanced traditional games such as casino games and lotteries. Given the fast-paced nature of the current global gambling market and industry, readers are advised to continue to stay familiar with up-to-date resources related to gambling legislation and policies.

Gambling Expansion and New Horizons

While the debate into the extent to which social media is a stand-alone industry remains open, other industries have clearly stepped up into the changing landscapes of online and Internet-friendly consumer spaces. For instance, cable companies are a thing of the past, with streaming options offered by Amazon, Netflix, Hulu, etc. The movie/entertainment industry adapted by offering movies online and using actors as social media influencers to promote upcoming movies. The gambling industry is no different and has adapted to changing landscapes and continues to thrive as one of the most profitable industries across the globe.

Gambling expansion is influenced by the intersection of technology advancements and accessibility variables (such as affordability and size of disposable income), interested industries looking to expand into uncharted horizons, and the socio-cultural values and preferences pertaining to the social responsibility of the industry and gamblers. In today's world, anyone who can access the Internet can access most forms of gambling, whether for money or for "free play," depending upon the jurisdiction. The promotion and accessibility of online and Internet gambling is clearly fuel for a wide range of booming global gambling markets including social gaming, sport betting or social casinos, and other traditional forms of gambling like casino and lottery games.

Online and Internet Gambling

Given the rise of accessibility and most countries' reliance on online and Internet-based technology, it is reasonable that the gambling industry has begun to make use of this space and industry. In some markets, societal shifts in accessibility and acceptability of online and Internet-based gaming options may have a direct impact on gambling revenue and subsequent losses. In the UK, online and Internet gambling or "remote gambling" is defined as "gambling in which persons participate by the use of remote communication [wherein communication means] using a) the internet, b) telephone, c) television, d) radio, or e) any other kind of electronic or other technology for facilitating communication" (Gambling Act, 2005, section 4 article 2(1)). In 2019, 55% of revenue collected from all forms of UK betting and gaming receipts were collected from remote gambling and lottery (HM Revenue & Customs, 2019).

Similarly, while the European market is one of the largest and most competitive online gambling markets, representing 49% of all online gambling platforms available across the globe in 2017, online gambling still only represents 20% of the overall gambling market across the European market (as compared to land-based gambling at 79.3%; see European Gambling and Betting Association, 2018). In the United Kingdom, comparatively, data analyzed from the British Gambling Prevalence Survey in 2010 on past-year gambling use reported 14% of the population gambled on the Internet (Wardle *et al.*, 2011), while online betting represented 37% of market shares and £5.3 billion total gross gambling yield in 2019 (Gambling Commission, 2019).

Countless other countries, such as Australia, Canada, and Southeast Asian nations including the Philippines and Cambodia, also share increases in popularity and use of online/Internet gambling (although the landscape of Southeast Asian nations is in flux regarding online gaming; see Hong, 2019). The United States has been slower to follow the online trend, with only 32% of states allowing some form of online gambling (e.g., sports betting, casino, poker, lottery) as of March 2020 (Legal US Online Gambling Guide, 2020).

Most patrons are drawn to online gambling for a slew of factors that brick-and-mortar establishments cannot provide. For instance, online gambling allows patrons to gamble with anonymity, enabling patrons to change their persona. Similarly, unlike brick-and-mortar establishments that have restricted business hours (i.e., closing hours) or "peak times" (e.g., casinos may be open 24/7, but table games are only open during "peak" times in areas of Nevada and other states), online gambling options are always available to play when desired. Such availability allows gamblers to chase their losses (return to the gambling activity after losing) at any time, without any social constraints on doing so. For example, a gambler who plays video poker at a casino may have difficulty returning the next day to chase their losses, as they would have to take time off work, travel to and from the casino, explain to other people why they returned so quickly, etc. However, the same gambler who plays video poker online may begin to chase their losses immediately after losing, as they would not have to take time off work to place additional bets and could continue to gamble while at work. The only thing that gambler needs is access to the Internet.

The fantasy world that online gambling establishes also allows patrons to use non-"real" money, with small distinctions in features between platforms that allow non-"real" money vs. pay-to-play platforms. The pay-to-play platforms are devoid of any in-the-moment money exchange (given that all monetary transactions take place through electronic mediums, patrons never interact or contact real money during the exchange). Free-to-play sites, conversely, allow patrons to play without any monetary exchange. While the convergence of the gaming and gambling worlds clearly collide with free-to-play sites, the space between social gaming and social gambling is very hard to see sometimes.

Social Gaming

Given the widespread availability of the Internet and corresponding technology needed to access the Internet, the new phenomenon of "social media" has spread like wildfire across the globe in recent years. Social media refers to websites or applications that allow users to communicate and share information with other individuals, groups, and/or organizations. With the advent of social media, new creative shared spaces were established where people should connect with others by sharing photos and comments, and even through playing games. Social media has helped to keep people connected and has come to represent an integral part of modern-day life.

The accessibility of online and other forms of easy-to-use technology (i.e., smartphone applications or "apps") has increased a market for free-to-play gambling-themed activities across a range of social media sites and applications. Social media platforms like Facebook play a major role in social gaming. Since 2004, social media applications have continued to grow in popularity, with a reported 3.2 billion users (or 42% of the global population) in 2019 (up 13% from 2018; Market.us, 2019).

Social media sites allow users an online space to communicate and share information with others, as well as a place to engage in entertainment-related activities, including playing games. Most social media users spend an average of two hours and 22 minutes per day on social media (Gilsenan, 2019). Further, 91% of users access social media platforms through mobile devices, and upwards of 80% of users' time spent on social media occurs through mobile platforms (which can only be accessed by a mobile device; see Lyfe Marketing, 2019).

Social gaming involves playing games that require no money or anything of monetary value to play, and no monetary payout is available. Further, gaming options are limitless and range from casino-themed games such as slot machines, table games such as blackjack and roulette or craps, to board/puzzle games (Words with Friends on Facebook; Candy Crush on smartphone apps) and multi-person challenge/competitive games with in-game social gaming features (e.g., World of Warcraft and Niantic's Pokemon Go). Social casinos, for instance, allow consumers to play any casino-type game for "free," and most are accessible through Facebook. While it is free to download or run the application and free to play portions of the game, there are in-game features that consumers can use real money towards, even though they will never get any money in return. Some users have ended up spending thousands of dollars within short time frames (e.g., PBS story on women who spent over $40,000 within nine months; PBS Newshour, 2019), which parallel similar patterns of problem gamblers.

Regardless of gaming theme or type of activity, features within aspects of social media provide 1) enhancement of self through instant gratification, 2) good use of time (particularly during episodes of boredom, loneliness, or other aversive or problematic situation to avoid), and unfortunately may also lead to 3) all-consuming thoughts and preoccupations with the games or other events that happened (or may happen). As such, social gaming (like other forms of gambling) may start as a form of entertainment, but when a client doesn't know what to do with boredom, engagement in social gaming activates the same part of the brain as more "addictive" activities like drugs, tobacco, and sexual activity, and subsequently ignites or maintains a pathway towards gambling addiction (see Chapter 2: Understanding Gambling Disorder for discussion on pathways model).

Two delineations have been made to distinguish social gaming from gambling. First, gaming is defined by its interactivity and dedicated reliance on skill-based play and programmed contextual features of progression or success (i.e., level progression throughout the game based on skill rather than only through chance). In contrast, gambling is defined by the financial or monetary betting and wagering on outcomes that are either by chance or by skill and result in potential to win prizes or money (King *et al.*, 2015). Free to play by definition is outside the legal bounds of "gambling," even though there are clear similarities between social gaming and Internet gambling.

When considered together, both entertainment activities share core features and commonalities. For instance, social gaming and free-to-play online platforms provide an environment for users to learn how to gamble so that when they play with their friends (either on alternative social media platforms or in brick-and-mortar establishments), they have the "skills" to be successful. Similarly, users on either social gaming or gambling sites can easily access the sites through the use of a smartphone, tablet, or computer.

Internet gamblers may be more likely to play social casino games than land-based gamblers (Gainsbury, Russell, & Hing, 2014).

Another core feature is the similarities in the use of digital advertising on social media to target social gaming and Internet gambling. In 2019, 73% of industry leaders surveyed believed social media marketing was "somewhat effective" and/or "very effective" for their business (Buffer, 2019). Moreover, in a study conducted by Gainsbury and colleagues in 2016, gamblers self-reported increased engagement in gambling following exposure to social media promotions targeting gambling (Gainsbury *et al.*, 2016).

Perhaps a more concerning commonality is the correlates between excessive gaming or gambling and the negative health and psychological wellbeing outcomes (e.g., Yau *et al.*, 2012; see also Chapter 2: Understanding Gambling Disorder for in-depth discussion of correlates of health and gambling and gaming disorder). The more common feature between gambling and gaming is the loss of control exhibited and reported by those impacted by the addition. While emerging evidence on the correlative relationships shared between gaming and gambling is relatively new and changing in real time, it is critical for therapists to always consider gaming as a potential threat to a client's overall health and wellbeing.

Sports Betting

The accessibility of online and other forms of remote gambling technology has influenced the prevalence of sports betting (see Winters & Deverensky, 2019). Sports betting in some Western countries has long been established and has seen dramatic increases in revenue thanks to the facilitation of online or Internet-based platforms. For instance, the United Kingdom has no restrictions on types of sports bets consumers can make (Gambling Act, 2005), and in 2019, the UK Gambling Commission oversaw 8320 betting shops throughout the country (Gambling Commission, 2019). Similarly, sports betting in the European markets is the most popular form of online gambling, comprising roughly 40% of all games played in 2017 (European Gaming and Betting Association, 2019). While most Western countries have historically allowed sports betting as a form of gambling entertainment, in other countries such as the United States, recent shifts in public policy have opened the door for the gaming industry to expand sports betting.

In the United States, the Professional and Amateur Sports Protection Act of 1992 (PASPA) made it illegal for states to authorize legal sports betting (except for a few states, like Nevada, who were grandfathered in being given pre-existing sports lotteries and sports betting frameworks; see also Gray, 2019). However, over time, socio-cultural support for sports gambling increased, with adults in various states in support of legalization. In May 2018, the US Supreme Court ruled that the 1992 ban on sports betting violated states' rights, and lifted PASPA, allowing the legalization of sports gambling to be the choice of individual states (de Vogue & Vazquez, 2018). Since that time, upwards of 15 states and counting, including the District of Columbia (Washington DC), have secured or are in the process of securing legislation to legalize sports betting. For instance, in June 2018, New Jersey became the third state to legalize sports betting, following Nevada and Delaware, with Pennsylvania, Rhode Island, and West Virginia close behind.

Regardless of jurisdiction, sports wagering continues to be easily accessible, and, as such, continues to increase patron engagement in placing bets (see also Estevez *et al.*, 2017). Online forms of sports wagering provide unique opportunities for the gambler to gamble 24 hours a day, 365 days a year, and to wager on anything imaginable when it comes to a sporting event. For instance, bets can be placed for more "traditional" sports wagers, where bets are placed on a specific outcome of the game or match before the game begins, with the outcome not determined until hours or days later. However, new forms of sports wagers, including in-play betting and micro-betting, allow patrons to place bets placed on outcomes that occur within the game or match with the outcome determined immediately or within a short time frame during the game (see Russell *et al.*, 2019). These newly established online sports gambling features, including live in-play betting, reduce the delay between wager and reward found in more traditional sports betting (Auer & Griffiths, 2013). For instance, during the 2020 Super Bowl football match in the United States, patrons could wager on anything from the overall winner, to gains/losses per quarter, to how long the singer took to sing the national anthem.

Consumer Protections and Harm Minimization to Promote Safe Gambling Use

Gambling can be and often remains a fun and exciting form of social enter-tainment for most individuals who play. For some, gambling is enjoyed at destination resort weekends in Las Vegas, or betting on a favorite sports team, or celebrating with friends by entering a poker tournament. For others, however, gambling can become an enigma in their day-to-day life, becoming all-encompassing to the extent that they no longer care about the negative consequences their gambling has on their overall quality of life (see also Chapter 2: Understanding Gambling Disorder for additional discussion of prevalence and comorbidity rates of problem and disordered gambling).

The gambling industry has historically been called to ensure consumer protections, most notably through safety measures and adopted programs specifically targeted to reduce gambling harm (i.e., responsible gambling (RG) programs). While the empirical evidence supporting most RG strat-egies is limited (Ladouceur *et al.*, 2017; Reilly, 2017), as countries continue to pursue legislative demands and requirements for gambling operations, there is continued pressure to provide RG initiatives and platforms to protect con-sumers (Williams, West, & Simpson, 2012). Common RG strategies across gambling types include self-exclusion, gambling behavior characteristics (including gambling expenditure, duration, and frequency), setting limits (related to gambling behavior characteristics), structural characteristics and features within the game of chance itself, and training staff and employees to recognize warning signs of problem gambling (Ladouceur *et al.*, 2017).

Self-Exclusion

Self-exclusion (SE, or voluntary exclusion) programs allow for the gambler to exclude themselves from specific gambling venues or areas (i.e., online providers). By participating in the programs, gamblers give up their rights to access the gambling venue or area; in most jurisdictions, gamblers can be penalized for trespassing or may face other charges if found on the premises. Often, gamblers can sign up at their preferred gambling venue or area, or by adhering to local processes for registration. Length of exclusion ranges from six months to one or five years, up to a lifetime, depending upon jurisdiction (Ladoucer *et al.*, 2017).

Self-exclusion programs have only been minimally researched compared to the numerous public policies that endorse or mandate their availability. To date, SE programs have been found to be used by younger adults (e.g., LaBrie *et al.*, 2007; Dragicevic *et al.*, 2015) and by middle-aged adults (LaBrie *et al.*, 2007; Nower & Blaszczynski, 2006). Younger and older males have been shown to be more likely to self-exclude faster than middle-aged males (Dragicevic *et al.*, 2015), while proximity and accessibility to gambling venues or areas has been argued to be a primary characteristic of those who self-exclude (LaBrie *et al.*, 2007). Engagement in self-exclusion has been shown to have a range of effects on behaviors and psychological functioning (Hayer & Meyer, 2010), including urges to gamble and perceived control over gambling to name a few (Ladouceur *et al.*, 2007; see also Ladouceur *et al.*, 2017 for review). However, a study by Nelson *et al.* (2010) showed that half of the 113 self-excluders followed for up to ten years after enrollment into the SE program attempted to enter a casino after enrollment. Clearly, the majority of the data collected is relatively dated, and focused primarily on brick-and-mortar gambling establishments. In the new era of online gambling, proximity to "games of chance" is now at your fingertips (i.e., smartphones, iPads, computer laptops, etc.). Additional research is needed to understand the utility of SE programs for online venues.

Family and friends of gamblers who begin to show signs of problem gambling cannot sign their loved one up for self-exclusion programs. The individual with a gambling problem must take the initiative to exclude. This essential feature ensures that when the gambler signs up, they take full responsibility not only for their choices and decision, but for their actions as well.

Game Features and Structural Characteristics

Most responsible gambling programs include specific game features and structural characteristics that promote responsible, safe gambling use. Common examples include warning messages, clock features, demo mode (to allow gamblers to play without using money), and pre-commitment for length of time or total money to wager (to name a few). Generally speaking,

RG programs allow gamblers to access information on healthy or "safe" gambling, in addition to information about erroneous gambling perceptions (i.e., probability of winning, independence of spins on a slot machine, etc.; see also Ladouceur *et al.*, 2017; Wohl *et al.*, 2013).

Research on responsible game features and structural characteristics to date have found promising, yet moderate, effects. For instance, warning messages placed in the middle of the gambling screens were reportedly more impactful and useful for gamblers than messages on the sides of the gambling screen (Gainsbury *et al.*, 2015), while messages using graphics (rather than text-only) in video lottery terminals were found to decrease behavioral intent to gamble when paired with messaging on family disruption (Munoz *et al.*, 2013). A more recent study (Blaszczynski, Gainsbury, & Karlov, 2014) evaluated a RG treatment package, including RG messaging, bank meters (feature allowing gambler to save their winnings in a "bank" to prevent re-gambling wins; banks can only be collected on termination of gambling play), alarm clocks (feature to allow gamblers to pre-set a specific amount of time to gamble, with an alarm signaling to gambler when duration is reached), demo mode (feature allowing gambler to watch game play without inserting money to do so), and charity donations (feature to allow gamblers to donate their money to charity instead of continued gambling). Researchers tested ten modified gaming machines across five Australian gambling venues, and subjected 300 gamblers to a structured interview on perceptions of gambling experience on the test machines, as well as direct observation. Interestingly, less than two-thirds (61%) of the sample reported noticing the new RG characteristics; 16% of the sample used the demo play before gambling with their money, with only 6% of those who used it doing so to take a break from gambling (the intended purpose of the feature); 61% of the sample did not notice the bank meter, with only 13.6% using the bank feature; 5.8% of the sample reported using the alarm clock, with only 5% of those who used it leaving the machine after the time had elapsed (the intended purpose of the feature); and the charity function was observed to be used "30% of the time with donations generally being less than one dollar" (Blaszczynski *et al.*, 2014, p.11).

Auer and Griffiths (2015) evaluated a responsible gambling program developed to provide personalized feedback to gamblers (i.e., Mentor) to online gamblers using a European online site. The Mentor system explored an opt-in system, where gamblers were provided with numerical, graphical, and textual forms of feedback on a range of gambling characteristics (i.e., bet size, time played, total wagered over 4–24-week period, etc.). When compared to no intervention control, gamblers who experienced the personalized feedback reduced the total amount of time and money gambled. Taken together, RG characteristics may need further refinement and personalized touches in order to increase the effectiveness of reducing harmful gambling use.

Gambling Behavior Characteristics

Gambling characteristics are an important aspect of providing behavior-based strategies for reducing harmful gambling use. However, not all gambling venues are created equal, which makes tracking gambling behaviors somewhat easy in some arenas (i.e., online and Internet-based venues), and somewhat complicated in other arenas (i.e., land-based venues). Behavioral characteristics include metrics for tracking gambling frequency (e.g., number of spins per day/week/month; number of times patron accesses gambling venue per day/week/month), gambling expenditure (i.e., total amount wagered during individual bets vs. expenditure by day/week/month), and gambling duration (i.e., amount of time spent gambling per day/week/month).

Research on gambling behavior characteristics is often established by using behavior-based algorithms to predict problem gambling, actual behavioral patterns of gamblers, and historical betting patterns to identify predictors for specific characteristics inherent to problem gambling (Ladouceur *et al.*, 2017). When taken together, evidence collected to date has established that total bets placed, number of active betting days, and duration of gambling, in addition to monetary variables (including magnitude of individual wagers and total net losses), may reliably identify problem gamblers, particularly those who play live-action sports betting (Gray *et al.*, 2012). Similar evidence reported by Braverman and colleagues (2013) showed that gamblers who engage in two or more types of gambling within the first few months of registering on the online betting platform bwin and those with high variability wagers in either casino or live-action sports gambling are more likely to benefit from RG programs when compared to gamblers with low variability wagers (as discussed by Ladouceur *et al.*, 2017, p.230).

Setting Limits

The goal for this RG strategy is to assist gamblers with using pre-commitment to develop pre-set limits to the amount of money or total time they *will* gamble. Pre-commitment strategies are successful given that they help the gambler set their own limits before coming into contact with the actual gambling game. Unfortunately, only a handful of studies have been published on this feature. Research published to date has found that voluntary limit setting for total amount of money wagered is more effective at reducing harmful gambling behavior (of lottery, casino, and poker players on an online gambling site) when compared to setting time limits (Auer & Griffiths, 2013). Voluntary self-limiting behavior of Internet gamblers was also found to reduce overall gambling activity when compared to gamblers who did not self-limit, but the total amount wagered per bet did not change (Nelson *et al.*, 2008).

Gambling operators have also explored global limit settings that are not voluntarily set *per se* by the gambler but are instead enforced within the game or activity itself. One particular approach has been to set limits on how much money gamblers can deposit into online gambling accounts. In one study, Broda and colleagues (2008) compared data from two years of actual sports gambling behavior records of 47,000 users of bwin and analyzed the differences between gamblers who exceeded pre-established limits and gamblers who did not. Interestingly, only 0.3% of the sample (n=160) exceeded deposit limits at least once throughout the two-year time frame. Furthermore, when authors compared gambling behavior before and after the limits were exceeded, they found that slightly more risky or unfavorable gambling behavior occurred after gamblers exceeded deposit limits.

While the area of setting limits is still in its infancy in terms of empirically validating the goals of these programs, there are mixed results indicating that reduction in money wagered or time played is mediated (or causally connected to) the inclusion of setting limits. Without empirical support that setting limits alone reduces gambling related harm, this approach should be conducted in conjunction with other harm-reduction intervention strategies (see Reilly, 2017; Ladouceur *et al.*, 2017).

Training Employees Who Interact with Gamblers

A more recent trend in RG strategies has been to focus on training gambling venue employees about the signs of problem gambling (e.g., LaPlante *et al.*, 2012; Delfabbro, Borgas, & King, 2012; Hing and Nuske, 2012; see also Ladoucer *et al.*, 2017). Employee trainings have centered on gambling awareness and problem gambling knowledge (LaPlante *et al.*, 2012), and how to help employees feel confident in discussing personal issues with gambling patrons (Hing & Nuske, 2012). Unfortunately, one study that explored the reliability of employees identifying problem gambling in patrons found that point-in-time employee ratings of potential problem gamblers were not accurate and were therefore not able to accurately identify problem gamblers (Delfabbro *et al.*, 2012).

Conclusion

Gambling is everywhere in today's society, and it doesn't look to be going anywhere, anytime soon. In fact, the gambling industry is not only thriving, but also growing. It is therefore reasonable to conclude that adults, children, families, and communities will increasingly be at risk for developing a problem with gambling. Given this unfortunate reality, it is our hope that the current text will:

- establish a clear, concise, and thoroughgoing analysis of gambling across the spectrum of severity, gaming characteristics, and modes of play
- provide a foundational knowledge for therapists in the human service professions (i.e., social work, psychology, counseling, marriage and family therapy, etc.) working with individuals at risk for or with problem gambling
- describe a working framework for understanding the etiology of problem gambling
- assist therapists in establishing case conceptualization strategies and specific treatment tools useful in gambling treatment.

In this way, the first section of the book will focus on the ecological (including neurological/biological, psychological, and sociological) and diagnostic factors correlative with problem gambling (Chapter 1: Gambling Is Everywhere; Chapter 2: Understanding Gambling Disorder), as well as research on the various evidence-informed clinical treatments or modes of interventions that have been shown to be efficacious (Chapter 3: Models of Intervention). The second section will provide readers with an in-depth, practical application for clinical settings that is useful in treating at-risk and problem gambling including general therapeutic overviews (Chapter 4: Models of Intervention—Applied; Chapter 5: Where to Start and What to Ask) and gambling-specific aspects of treatment (Chapter 6: Harm-Reduction Approaches across the Continuum; Chapter 7: Finances; Chapter 8: Family; Chapter 9: Self-Help and Peer Supports; and Chapter 10: The Legal System and Gambling).

CHAPTER 2

UNDERSTANDING GAMBLING DISORDER

Pathways towards Etiology, Prevalence, and Comorbid Determinants of Health

"Addiction lives in the space of repeating old behaviors in hopes of getting new outcomes."

Gambling is a socially acceptable and legal form of entertainment present in cultures throughout the world (Ladouceur *et al.*, 2002). In 2020, it is easier to access gambling activities and place a wager across the globe than ever before. As discussed in Chapter 1: Gambling Is Everywhere, the types of gambling venues or arenas appear endless, with novel forms of gambling activities emerging at such a fast pace that it is challenging for researchers, policy makers, and therapists to keep up.

Given the array of gambling venues, arenas, and game options available, it is often important to consider the spectrum of use severity in order to develop more conceptually concise frameworks for how individuals may come to develop a gambling problem or addiction. In common with most behavioral or substance-use addictions, gambling also can be considered across a use continuum from *experimental or recreational use* (i.e., gambling as a way to "see what happens" or as a form of social entertainment with friends or family, with longer periods of time between uses), *at-risk use* (i.e., gambling as a way to cope with life stressors, preoccupation with gambling during non-gambling periods, chasing or returning to the gambling venue soon after losing), to *problematic* or *harmful use* (i.e., gambling regardless of negative consequences of doing so, loss of meaningful social relationships, increased suicidality and other mental health conditions like depression). Problematic or harmful use (i.e., gambling disorder) can also be considered across a continuum from excessive to compulsive or problem to disordered gambling (see also Bellegarde & Potenza, 2010).

According to the Diagnostic Statistical Manual (DSM-5; American Psychiatric Association, 2013) and the International Statistical Classification of Diseases and Related Health Problems (ICD-10; World Health Organization, 2018), gambling disorder is characterized by the presence of repeated unsuccessful attempts to quit or reduce one's gambling, preoccupation with gambling (including reliving past gambling experiences, rumination on future gambling experiences, thinking about ways to get money to gamble, etc.), and lying or concealing one's gambling behavior (see Chapter 5: Where to Start and What to Ask for more in-depth discussion and classification of DSM and ICD-10 diagnostic criteria for disordered gambling). Individuals who meet criteria for "disordered gambling" may also report tolerance (i.e., needing to spend larger amounts of money or gamble for longer periods of time to experience similar effects; Toce-Gerstein, Gerstein, & Volberg, 2003) and withdrawal symptoms during periods of abstinence from gambling (Shaffer, 1997; Wareham & Potenza, 2010).

Given the severity continuum, combined with the agreement among the global addiction community on symptoms associated with more severe (or disordered) gambling, it is clear that problem and pathological gamblers represent a heterogeneous population, and, as such, treatments should not follow a one-size-fits-all approach (see Ladouceur, Lachance, & Fournier, 2009). In order to provide effective gambling treatments that are idiosyncratic for each gambler seeking treatment, researchers have been focused on determining etiological risk factors (those that make individuals more likely to develop a gambling problem) and protective factors (those that make individuals less likely to develop a gambling problem).

Therefore, the purpose of the current chapter is to take a deep dive into the current research base related to the etiology of gambling addiction.

Our goal is to outline 1) how gambling impacts the *whole person* (including biological, psychological, social, and spiritual variables), 2) the comorbidity of gambling with other mental health conditions generally and substance-use disorders specifically, and 3) a clear working framework for gambling symptomology and classification of gambling pathways that is useful for therapists when developing treatment plans. It is important to note that the majority of empirical evidence reported in the current chapter has been conducted in Canada and the United States, with moderate representation of populations in Europe, Australia, and Asia (see also Stucki & Rihs-Middel (2007) and Calado & Griffiths (2016) for similar observations of population-based research on gambling). Given this, we strongly suggest the reader consider the conclusions and implications drawn from research outcomes in conjunction with aspects related to minority groups and/or under-represented sub-populations. Similarly, we also suggest readers continue to stay updated with research findings as they emerge.

Etiological Predictors and Risk Factors for Developing Gambling Disorder

Gambling prevalence rates fluctuate across the globe. In Western nations, recreational gambling (or gambling for entertainment purposes only) tends to fluctuate from 41% of adult populations (e.g., Greece 2014; Economou *et al.*, 2019) to 78% of the adult population (United States 2018; Volberg, McNamara, & Carris, 2018). Problem and disordered gambling prevalence rates, on the other hand, have been reported between 2.2% and 5.8% of adults (United States; Kessler *et al.*, 2008; Williams, Volberg, & Stevens, 2012; Calado & Griffiths, 2016). Recent systematic reviews of prevalence studies report between 0.12% and 5.8% of past-year problem gambling rates globally, with estimated 0.12–3.4% in Europe specifically (Calado & Griffiths, 2016). Similarly, indirect measures of problem or disordered gambling have also begun to emerge. For example, data from hospital admissions reports from the National Health Service in the United Kingdom showed gambling-related hospital admissions more than doubled between 2015 and 2018 (Busby, 2019).

Research collected over the last 40 years continues to make it clear that gambling problems do not affect all individuals who gamble and may not be consistent across etiological factors (Welte *et al.*, 2001). Given the accessibility of gambling establishments and online venues, combined with the prevalence rates of recreational gambling use across the globe, it is unclear why only some individuals who gamble develop a gambling problem? Are some people just born to be impulsive or have "addictive personalities"? Does addiction serve some sort of evolutionary advantage, and therefore continue to be passed on generation to generation? Is it the environment that produces addictions, such as home life or parenting styles? Is the biology or genes of the person important for developing a gambling problem? If addiction in general, and gambling addiction more specifically, isn't evolutionarily advantageous (which we'd argue it isn't), and if there isn't any pro-social aspect to developing and maintaining one's gambling addiction, then why does it continue to affect individuals, families, and communities?

At bottom, if we consider addictions like a state (rather than a trait or similar conceptualized deficit), then we can consider ways to influence behavioral change so that the person can be successful in recovery. Some theoretical perspectives argue that addiction is a disease of the brain, suggesting that the neural pathways of executive function become distorted and motivational processes become amplified as a consequence of the interaction between behaviors and their effects on the brain (e.g., West & Brown, 2013). Other theoretical perspectives argue that addiction is controlled by respondent conditioning and operant learning paradigms, such as emotional conditioning, and schedules of reinforcement, all of which points to environmental factors and variables that form the etiology of addiction (see also Silverman *et al.*, 2011). While genetic predispositions for developing gambling disorders are evident, it is important to consider biological *and* environmental and socio-cultural factors that influence the etiology of gambling disorders. Further, psychological, biological, and familial aspects of problem gambling, alone, are not sufficient to explain differences in rates of problem and disordered gambling among different cultural groups (see also Raylu & Oei, 2004).

More comprehensive frameworks incorporate biological/neurological and environmental models (to include both psychological and socio-cultural factors) to help understand and conceptualize multifaceted disparities across heterogeneous populations (i.e., biopsychosocial framework; Sharpe, 2002;

Sharpe & Tarrier, 1993). Primary areas of emphasis within a biopsychosocial framework include biological/neurological factors, psychological factors (including behavioral and cognitive factors), sociological factors, and, more recently, spiritual factors (i.e., Katerndahl, 2008). In order to understand the complexity of how gambling disorders are established, it is important to consider the whole person (e.g., biological, psychological, socio-cultural, and spiritual factors).

Biological/Neurological Implications

Neurobiological models of gambling disorder follow similar models to those used in drug and alcohol addiction (see also Potenza, 2008), and typically include one of four areas of scientific research: 1) genetic investigations of gene patterns, 2) biochemical studies on the chemical processes that occur, 3) functional neuroimaging studies that study how the brain functions, and 4) psychological and pharmacological treatment interventions based on the biological and neurological factors (Grant, Brewer, & Potenza, 2006).

In a systematic review of genetic studies published before September 2012, Gyollai and colleagues (2014) found a handful of studies that identified associations between gambling disorder and dopaminergic and serotonergic systems. Both serotonin and dopamine pathways have been found to be essential components within behavioral control and reinforcement learning processes related to drug and non-drug reward pathways (Wareham & Potenza, 2010). For instance, dopamine has been implicated as a primary neurotransmitter within the reward center of the brain responsible for reinforcing behaviors (including drug/alcohol/gambling use, eating food, having sex, shopping, etc.). Following engagement in a specific behavior, dopamine is produced wherein the prefrontal cortex is signaled as a way for the brain to identify reinforcing vs. aversive stimulation. In other words, after engaging in a specific behavior that activates release of dopamine, that release signals to the prefrontal cortex to do more of that behavior to release more dopamine (essentially creating a "feedback loop"). It is believed that the associative learning between cues, behaviors, reward schedules, and the release of dopamine influences the motivation processes that can override cognitive control (or self-control). A handful of studies have shown a positive association between dopamine D2 receptor gene (DRD2) and disordered gambling (see review by Gyollai *et al.*, 2014). Furthermore, dopamine transmission can decrease sensitivity to rewarding or pleasurable experiences. In this way, given the repeated exposure to dopaminergic activation, the gambler may begin to habituate to those functions and become insensitive to the system itself (i.e., the actual reward), and therefore continue to engage in more and more gambling to seek a rewarding outcome (see also Goudriaan, 2011).

Serotonin, on the other hand, has been shown to regulate behavioral inhibition (or the tendency to avoid novel or aversive stimulation) and behavioral cessation (stopping engagement in a specific behavior), and in some cases has been shown to function in punishment-induced inhibition (Crockett, Clark, & Robbins, 2009). Interestingly, gamblers have been found to have low levels of serotonin and display different behavioral and biochemical responses to serotonergic drugs than age-matched controls (see review by Gyollai *et al.*, 2014).

In addition to genetic research, neurobiological research studies have sought to determine physiological aspects related to addiction in general and gambling specifically. Functional magnetic resonance imaging (fMRI) measures hemodynamic changes following neuronal activity, and has been a widely used technology for analyzing global brain functioning and maladaptive patterns particularly within substance-use research (Suckling & Nestor, 2017). The vascular system supplies energy required for maintaining neuronal networks when blood oxygenation levels change as blood becomes deoxygenated after neuronal activity (Huettel, Song, & McCarthy, 2009). This technique uses magnetic fields and the magnetic properties of hemoglobin to produce brain images through a technique called "blood-oxygen-levels-dependent" (BOLD) imaging. When blood is oxygenated, it is less magnetic, and the fMRI machine is designed to detect these differences. To date, fMRI studies have found decreased ventral cortex activation (dopaminergic system) in disordered gamblers when compared with controls (e.g., Potenza, Leung, *et al.*, 2003; Potenza, Steinberg, *et al.*, 2003; Reuter *et al.*, 2005), and dopaminergic differences between disordered gamblers and non-disordered gamblers during near-miss outcomes and winning outcomes (Habib & Dixon, 2010) and compared to large vs. small wins (Dixon, Wilson, & Habib, 2015). Further, fMRI studies have found similarities and differences in brain activation patterns of disordered gamblers and individuals with substance-use disorders (Wareham & Potenza, 2010).

Another common neurological consequence that occurs following high-frequency behavioral repetition is neuroadaptation (or the change in neuronal function as a result of prior repetitive experiences; see also Shaffer & Kidman, 2003). Tolerance, for instance, requires that the user increase the dose to experience a similar outcome following use; in the same way, disordered gamblers increase bet size and/or duration of gambling play in order to achieve the same level of excitement or arousal (Shaffer & Kidman, 2003; Dixon, Wilson, & Habib, 2015). Withdrawal is also considered an example of neuroadaptation and has been found to occur in a range of substance-use disorders including gambling (Potenza, 2006).

Psychological Implications

Psychological factors have been shown to influence disordered gambling generally, and gambling behavioral characteristics specifically. Common psychological factors that have been found to be associated with problem and disordered gambling include chasing losses, continuing to gamble even when experiencing negative consequences (Potenza, 2006), impulsive choice making (Bellegrade & Potenza, 2010; Petry, 2001), irrational beliefs or thoughts about gambling including superstitions about games of chance or related illusions of control (e.g. Dixon, Hayes, & Aban, 2000; Langer, 1975).

Chasing losses, or continued gambling to get back monies lost, reflects an individual's preoccupation with gambling and potential correlation with irrational beliefs about winning (Griffiths & Whitty, 2010). Chasing wins, on the other hand, can also occur, wherein the person continues to gamble to chase after a larger win. Chasing has been considered a significant behavioral marker of problem and disordered gambling (Gainsbury, Suhonen, & Saastamoinen, 2014), even though chasing has also been observed in recreational gamblers (Dickerson, Hinchy, & Fabre, 1987). Interestingly, chasing losses has been conceptualized as playing a major role in the persistence of gambling, particularly in the presence of negative consequences (e.g., Blaszczynski & Nower, 2002).

Impulsivity (or impaired impulse control) is considered a behavioral pattern wherein individuals behave in ways that result in more immediate (often only slightly reinforcing or preferred) consequences rather than those that result in more delayed (yet often more likely to be highly reinforcing or preferred) consequences. Impulsive behaviors are often described as reactions to internal or external stimuli, often with little regard for the potential negative consequences of the behavior (Moeller *et al.*, 2001; Bellegrade & Potenza, 2010). Deficits or impaired impulse control has also been established as a risk factor for developing problem or disordered gambling (Bellegrade & Potenza, 2010; Petry, 2001; Goudriaan, 2011), and has been found to be associated with harm avoidance (Potenza, 2007).

Irrational beliefs, such as superstitions and illusions of control, also play a role in determining psychological factors of problem and disordered gambling. For instance, the gambler's fallacy is the belief that outcomes of random events will balance over time, even though each individual outcome is independent of the next. Examples of gambler's fallacies have been shown in lottery play (Clotfelter & Cook, 1993), pari-mutuel games (Terrell, 1994), casino games (Croson & Sundali, 2005), and blackjack (Glassford, Wilson, & Gupta, 2020). Similar is the illusion of control (Langer, 1975) or a belief that a decision or action may change the probability of winning even though there is no actual change in the outcome (Maclin, Dixon, & Hayes, 1999). For example, a gambler may operate under the rule "If I hit the bet button hard, the machine wins" or "Betting on black hits more than betting on numbers in roulette," and may continue to gamble even during a string of negative outcomes or losses in hopes that the held belief will come through. Even further, if a gambler learns that another person either won a large sum of money or if gamblers become aware that another person won because of their control of the outcome, gamblers will engage in more risky bets (Martinez *et al.*, 2011).

Socio-Cultural Implications

Social and cultural factors that play a role in problem and disordered gambling involve aspects of individual, familial, and community-based factors or variables. Factors that blend both biological and socio-cultural aspects, such as race/ethnicity, age (particularly age of onset for first gambling exposure), and gender, have also been found to have divergent effects on prevalence rates for problem and disordered gambling (see also Petry, 2005). For instance, research suggests that racial and ethnic minorities are more likely to develop a gambling disorder, with prevalence rates of minority groups higher than that of non-minority groups (Alegría *et al.*, 2010).

Across gambling subtypes, the age of first gambling experience (or age of onset) has been found to be associated with gambling severity (Kessler *et al.*, 2008; Rahman *et al.*, 2012), and worsened treatment outcomes (Jiménez-Murcia *et al.*, 2010). Previous research on adolescent risk factors in the development of gambling disorders estimates upwards of 15% of youth develop a gambling problem (Canada sample; Derevensky & Gupta, 2004). Gender differences, interestingly, are also impacted by age of onset. While some studies report that males are almost two times more likely to develop a gambling problem than females (Welte *et al.*, 2003), females have higher probability of developing a gambling problem later in life when compared to males of the same age (Boughton & Falenchuk, 2007).

Sexual preference and sexual identity, including ascription outside of a binary sexual orientation (i.e., gay, lesbian, bisexual, trans/pansexual, etc.), has been associated with increased propensity to develop problem gambling within college student-athletes (Canadian sample; Richard *et al.*, 2019), and with gender-diverse 9th and 11th graders (United States sample; Rider *et al.*, 2019). Of particular note is the finding that "trandsgender youth assigned to male at birth [are] at risk for gambling involvement and problem gambling," while "transgendered youth assigned to female at birth also reported higher rates of problem gambling than both cisgender youth assigned male and female at birth" (Rider *et al.*, 2019, p.79).

To date, moderate attention has been paid to specific research into the influential role of culture in the development of problem and disordered gambling. Familial factors such as divorce history (Black *et al.*, 2012), socioeconomic status (Welte *et al.*, 2004), and domestic violence (Gerstein *et al.*, 1999) have been found to influence prevalence of problem and disordered gambling.

For every problematic gambler, individuals in the gambler's community are negatively impacted (Lobsinger & Beckett, 1996) through societal costs such as unpaid debts and bankruptcies (Ladouceur *et al.*, 1994), and increased criminal activity (Single *et al.*, 2003).

When considering cultural influences, research in the United States has focused on immigrant status as a mediating factor. For example, Cambodian refugees living in Long Beach, California (Marshall, Elliott, & Schell, 2009) and Southeast Asian refugees and immigrants living in the United States (Petry *et al.*, 2003) have been found to have higher rates of problem or disordered gambling when compared to the majority group. On the other hand, when immigrant status is compared across first-generation, second-generation, third-generation, and non-immigrant status, the prevalence of gambling and problem gambling has been shown to be lower among first-generation immigrants than native-born adults in the United States (Wilson *et al.*, 2015). Interestingly, however, second-generation immigrants and non-immigrants were more likely to report problem gambling compared to first-generation immigrants (Wilson *et al.*, 2015).

Another cultural feature pertains to how individuals gamble; the type of gambling activity enjoyed and played by patrons often comes with unequal risks for developing problem or disordered gambling. For instance, some studies show the greatest predictor of problem gambling is past-year gambling on the Internet (Volberg *et al.*, 2018; Wood *et al.*, 2007; Griffiths & Barnes, 2008; Griffiths *et al.*, 2009; Wood and Williams, 2011; Gainsbury *et al.*, 2014) or mobile devices (Gainsbury *et al.*, 2016). Perhaps not shockingly, most gamblers who gamble online also gamble across multiple different gambling platforms, including offline or brick-and-mortar establishments (Wardle *et al.*, 2011). Sports betting, similar to online gambling, has also been associated with higher prevalence rates of problem and disordered gambling (Hing, Russell, & Browne, 2017). Interestingly, there are increasing numbers of young males seeking treatment for sports betting (e.g., Blaszczynski & Hunt, 2011).

Spiritual Implications

Spirituality has many definitions, but is often described as a universal human experience that includes a connection with aspects of life that are bigger than oneself; typically, some aspect of searching for meaning, growth, transcendental and personal experiences of existence, etc. It is important for therapists to realize that spirituality is not the same as religion; spirituality commonly refers to non-dogmatic aspects of human experience, whereas religion commonly refers to a specific, often dogmatic, particular practice to enhance the human experience (i.e., Christianity, Islam, Judaism, Buddhism, Daoism, etc.). Engagement in spirituality has been shown to lower suicide risk in women (VanderWeele *et al.*, 2016), and may protect against major depression (Miller *et al.*, 2014).

Spirituality research in addiction work began to take shape through research on pathways to recovery, and attention to the "lived experiences" of individuals in recovery (Jordan & Morgan, 2012). Common application of spirituality in treatment/recovery is often attributed to Alcoholics Anonymous (AA). A central tenet of recovery in AA is the notion of spirituality (Kurtz, 1986), and this is often discussed in the context of a spiritual component within recovery that often leads to phenomena including "surrender" and "conversion" (Jordan & Morgan, 2012, p.13). From a spirituality perspective, "something" happens that helps to shape the individual's way of thinking, feeling, and behaving in regard to recovery; the "something" that helps individuals get and stay clean is often of spiritual/religious emphasis (Jordan & Morgan, 2012).

Unlike AA, however, Gamblers Anonymous (GA) takes a divergent approach. While both AA and GA adhere to a 12-Step model, daily/weekly meetings for both the individual suffering from the addiction as well as family members (i.e., Alanon, Gamanon) and view gambling as a disease that is to be arrested through abstinence rather than cured, there are very stark and contrasting differences as well.

First, GA uses the word "spiritual" as one to describe characteristics of the human mind that represent human qualities of kindness, generosity, honesty, and humility. There is no mention of a "spiritual awakening" in GA. Often, disordered gamblers report religious affiliation toward gambling, including sanction or endorsed participation, superstitious beliefs (i.e., praying to win, rituals believed to help wins occur and religious medallions as "lucky charms"). Furthermore, gamblers may report feeling more (or less) spiritual or "closer to God" as they win and lose, therefore reinforcing irrational beliefs and cognitive distortions about God "helping them win." In this way, the message of "hope" is vital to GA, as it is not "God" or a deity alone who will grant one's "good fortune" or "luck."

Second, GA offers longer meetings (2+ hours vs. standard 1-hour meeting time for AA) and sporadic sponsorship rather than strict adherence to a sponsor model. Similarly, GA recognizes "clean" time whereas AA/NA (Narcotics Anonymous) recognize "recovery" time. GA focuses on patience and a "normal way of thinking and living" whereas AA/NA focus on "delayed gratification" and "restoration to sanity" (see also Browne, 1994).

While research on gambling and religious affiliations (such as Islamic, Buddhist, and Jewish affiliation) is sparse, previous research has shown positive associations with gambling involvement and affiliation with Christian sects, including Catholicism (Walker, 1992; Grichting, 1986). Similarly, research has found positive factors such as spirituality and similar "recovery capital" (i.e., any factor that functions as an advantage for individuals during recovery) share positive associations with gambling symptom improvement (Gavriel-Fried, Moretta, & Potenza, 2020). However, one study found that spirituality may actually function differently between younger and older adult gamblers, as positive correlations between recovery capital and spirituality was only identified with younger adults (Gavriel-Fried, Moretta, & Potenza, 2020).

Taken together, it is clear that gambling disorder is not a "weakness of the will" or a "choice" that gamblers make. From a biopsychosocial-spiritual perspective, gambling disorder is a result of a myriad of factors; between the altered neuronal networks that develop following repeated use to the ease of accessibility and cultural acceptability, the consequences of a person's gambling impacts the whole person, and interpersonal and socio-cultural gambling impacts the whole person. Understanding how each of these factors can influence a person to develop a problem with gambling is where we turn to next.

Pathways Model of Problem Gambling

As previously mentioned, gamblers may start out as recreational users and, over time, may begin to develop a problem with gambling given an array of potential biopsychosocial risk factors. The progression from "recreational gambler" to "disordered gambler" is beginning to be better understood; however, there are only a few conceptual models that appear promising in understanding how gambling disorder develops across gambling subtypes.

Perhaps most notable is the pathways model set forth by Blaszczynski and Nower (2002). The pathways model provides a conceptual synthesis between biological, psychological, socio-cultural, and spiritual determinants of problem gambling (Milosevic & Ledgerwood, 2010). The model also provides a way for therapists to consider characteristics and emotional and biological vulnerabilities as a way to conceptualize the "type" of gambler profile and treat the whole person during intervention (Valleur *et al.*, 2016). In this way, gamblers can be considered as a heterogeneous population, wherein not every gambler will present with the same history or activation of a problem with gambling (i.e., emotional vulnerabilities or impulsive traits). Those who seek treatment should therefore be provided one designed specifically for their idiosyncratic biological, psychological, and ecological traits in some capacity.

According to the pathways model, all problem and disordered gambling starts by way of *ecological determinants,* or the availability and ease of access that have long been associated with higher prevalence of problem and disordered gambling. Research conducted to date continues to show that access to gambling facilities increases the likelihood for gambling disorders (St-Pierre *et al.*, 2014). The closer a person is to a gambling venue or establishment, the more likely they are to gamble.

The subsequent pathways present themselves differently depending upon the three categorizations: behaviorally conditioned problem gamblers, psychologically vulnerable problem gamblers, and antisocial and impulsive problem gamblers.

Behaviorally Conditioned Gamblers

The first subtype incorporates the general model for how gambling disorders can be developed. Following ecological factors, behaviorally conditioned gamblers fall susceptible to classical and operant conditioning (including schedules of reinforcement and conditioned responding), habituation (decreased exhibitory responses over time), and chasing losses. Gamblers within this subtype are not impacted by a psychiatric pathology or biological vulnerabilities; instead, they fall to the addictive reinforcement schedule of gambling in general (Blaszczynski & Nower, 2002).

Behaviorally conditioned gamblers are also influenced by the *classical and operant conditioning* processes that result in the "development of habitual patterns of gambling and cognitive process resulting in faulty beliefs related to personal skill and probability of winning" (Blaszczynski & Nower, 2002, p.491). Learning paradigms, like classical conditioning (i.e., Ivan Pavlov's conditioning with dogs, associative learning) and operant conditioning (i.e., Edward Thorndike's cat mazes, B.F. Skinner's operant rat and pigeon chambers, consequential learning), are employed in most gambling activities. For instance, an example of operant conditioning is the intermittent and variable reinforcement schedules; some games of chance are random, while others are based on odds or level of skill. Regardless, the reinforcement schedule is established so that *sometimes* the gambler receives a reinforcer (i.e., a winning outcome), and sometimes the gambler does not. The intermittent nature of sometimes receiving a reinforcer is what makes the reinforcement schedule so potent, as it increases the likelihood that the gambler will continue to gamble in the future. Additionally, gambling may provide the gambler a form of negative reinforcement, wherein aversive experiences (such as anxiety, stress, or depression) are reduced or seem to "go away" as a result of gambling; over time, the escape and avoidance reinforcer that the gambler receives from gambling during aversive situations increases the likelihood of more gambling in the future. Similarly, behaviorally conditioned gamblers will report biased or distorted thoughts and belief systems associated with gambling. Common gambling-related cognitive schemas include the illusion of control (e.g., belief systems wherein the gambler believes they can "beat" the odds of winning or somehow skew randomness in their favor to win), gambler's fallacy (e.g., perceptions and superstitious thinking related to probability theory), and similar distorted or irrational belief structures that increase the gambler's involvement and engagement in gambling.

Patterns labeled *habituation* emerge as a result of an associative and instrumental-learning paradigm. Habituation occurs when a physiological or arousal response is diminished following repeated exposure to a stimulus. In this way, as individuals continue to gamble and are exposed to gambling-related stimuli (including cognitive biases, game insignia and slogans, win and loss outcomes, etc.), their arousal level drops significantly over repeated exposure, and additional gambling is needed to experience similar "highs" (or arousal levels). *Chasing* losses (or wins) is another residual developed from conditioning paradigms. With chasing, individuals persist with gambling engagement even in the presence of negative consequences/outcomes.

While research on the pathways model continues to emerge (e.g., Moon *et al.*, 2017), gamblers within this subtype tend to report less severe gambling-related problems and do not show signs of more severe psychiatric or mental health disorders including co-occurring substance use/abuse, impulsivity, or other symptoms of psychopathology (Blaszczynski & Nower, 2002).

Psychologically Vulnerable Gamblers

The second subtype incorporates ecological factors, emotional and biological vulnerabilities factors, classical and operant conditioning, habituation, and chasing. Gamblers within this subtype have biological and emotional vulnerabilities to experiencing a range of mental health considerations (including mood disturbances, depression/anxiety, substance abuse), history of engaging in maladaptive coping or problem-solving skills (including risk-taking, poly substance use, negative reactions to life stressors and events), and negative family background experiences. In contrast to behaviorally conditioned gamblers, psychologically vulnerable gamblers are more likely to use gambling to relieve aversive states (i.e., escape-based gamblers), rather than to gamble as a form of entertainment. Further, emotional vulnerabilities require additional treatment approaches to address the co-occurring vulnerabilities as well as the gambling disorder (Blaszczynski & Nower, 2002, p.494).

Antisocial and Impulsive Gamblers

The third subtype incorporates ecological factors, emotional and biological vulnerabilities factors, impulsive traits, classical and operant conditioning, habituation, and chasing. Gamblers within this subtype have similar emotional and biological vulnerabilities but are distinguishable from other subtypes given features of impulsivity, antisocial personality, and attention deficit. Given the multidimensional histories of this subgroup with impulsivity and antisocial personality tendencies, gamblers are more likely to engage in an array of behaviors in addition to their gambling that may inflict harm on themselves or others, including suicidality, low tolerance for boredom, criminality, substance use/abuse, and irritability (Blaszczynski & Nower, 2002). Take, for instance, the high correlation between problem gambling and attention deficit hyperactivity disorder (ADHD). Problem gamblers are estimated to be four times more likely to have a diagnosis of ADHD than the general population (Theule *et al.*, 2019). Other studies have supported that upwards of 25% of treatment-seeking gamblers sampled present with ADHD (Waluk, Youssef, & Dowling, 2016; Peter *et al.*, 2016). Further, research also supports a positive relationship between childhood ADHD and problem gambling later in life, particularly when childhood ADHD persists into adulthood (Chamberlain *et al.*, 2015). Given the biological and emotional vulnerabilities, in addition to the impulsive tendencies, it is theorized that the gambling problem itself is independent of the impulsivity and antisocial traits, and is therefore a good predictor for increased severity of problem gambling (Blaszczynski & Nower, 2002).

Considerations for Special Populations and Gambling

Adolescents

Adolescent prevalence rates of problem gambling continue to rise (Jacobs, 2000), with recent estimates as high as 12.3% (European sample derived by systematic review; Calado, Alexandre, & Griffiths, 2017). Adolescents may be more susceptible to developing problem gambling given the correlation between parental gambling and increased probability of adolescent gambling (Gupta & Derevensky, 1997), and more vulnerable to negative consequences (Griffiths & Wood, 2000). Further, given modern forms of today's technology, some argue that adolescents may be more susceptible given the similarities between technology-based games and gambling activities (Delfabbro *et al.*, 2009), not to mention the explosion of gambling expansion over the past decade (see also Gupta & Derevensky, 2000a).

Adolescents with gambling problems are more likely to be male than female (Ellenbogen, Derevensky, & Gupta, 2007), and range from 16 to 25 years of age. Similarly, adolescents are more likely to start gambling at an earlier age (sometimes as early as eight years old), have experienced a big win early in their gambling history, consistently chase losses, started gambling with their parents or by themselves, and experience emotional states (i.e., depression, excitement, or arousal) before or during gambling. Adolescents with problem gambling are also more likely to have difficulties in school (often exhibited by poor grades, truancy, history of delinquency, and lower self-esteem than their peers), and engage in other "risky" behaviors (including drug/alcohol use, smoking, stealing money to gamble, etc.) (Griffiths & Wood, 2000, p.208). Finally, similar to adult patterns of at-risk and problematic gambling, adolescents are also influenced by cultural background (Ellenbogen, Gupta, & Derevensky, 2007).

While the majority of these symptoms mirror more common challenges of development, and can therefore be ascribed to "typical teenage behavior" by parents, warning signs include sudden changes in personality (such as changes in mood or attitudes, lying about what they've been doing), changes in standards of schoolwork, loss of interest in preferred activities, changes in concentration, and money and/or expensive possessions going missing (Griffiths & Wood, 2000). The pathways model is also a useful tool to determine the gambling subtype of adolescent gamblers (Nower & Blaszczynski, 2004).

Older Adults

Older adults refers to people aged 65 or older, and current estimates of older adults are upwards of 8.5% of the global population and are projected to jump to 17% of the world's population by 2050 (He, Goodkind, & Kowal, 2015). This subpopulation is an important market for the gambling industry, given the opportunity and leisure time of older adults on a daily basis (due to retirement age), and disposable income. The gambling industry puts big money each year into marketing efforts to target older adults to gamble at various establishments. Examples of marketing efforts include targeted offers to senior centers and retirement communities; free or reduced-cost buses to get to gambling venues; discounted food and/or other forms of entertainment; and sometimes gifts or giveaways (e.g., 12-piece luggage sets, new cars, etc.). In prevalence studies on gambling and older adults, 77% of older adults report gambling at least once in the previous year (Wiebe, 2000).

Often, older adults enjoy gambling particularly as a form of leisure, as it provides them with an opportunity to socialize with others outside of their home (McNeilly & Burke, 2000), provides a way for them to use and maintain cognitive skills, and may promote some physical activity depending upon the amount of walking or other movement used to reach the site. While older adults are usually not associated with high prevalence rates of disordered gambling, some research indicates that older adults experience severe physical, emotional, and psychological comorbidity rates (Van der Maas *et al.*, 2017).

When working with older adults, therapists can take two different approaches: direct or indirect. A direct approach is when therapists conduct workshops or trainings specifically about problem gambling, including strategies for keeping gambling fun, and providing resources for getting help. An indirect approach is when therapists conduct workshops or trainings about health and wellness during retirement years, and indirectly or passively target gambling activities. Either approach works best with strong staff support, including activities coordinators, recreational therapists, case/care managers, service coordinators, senior-level management, social workers, and other medical professionals who interact with older adults.

Of particular concern when working with any client, and in particular older adults given that they are prescribed more medications than any other age group, is the link between prescriptions for dopamine agonists (drugs used to treat Parkinson's disease and restless leg syndrome) and the association with side effects of excessive gambling and other impulse control disorders including hypersexuality and compulsive shopping (Moore, Glenmullen, & Mattison, 2014). Research to date has identified a link between dopamine agonists in patients with Parkinson's disease and development of disordered gambling (Tippmann-Peikert, Park, *et al.*, 2007; Potenza, Voon, & Weintraub, 2007; Weintraub *et al.*, 2010).

Diverse Communities

Diverse communities, based on differences in characteristics including cultural and racial backgrounds, age, gender/sex, etc., may not seek clinical services in similar ways or at all, and may subsequently be under-represented in gambling research and/or in clinical treatment. When working with gamblers from diverse communities, therapists should always be mindful and aware of their own cultural "self," and how their cultural "self" engages with the client and the client's family and other cultural "selves." Similarly, integration of cultural contextual considerations during treatment, with an eye towards gambling awareness and prevention across cultures (different cultures and cultural "selves" require different messaging), will be helpful to achieve quality rapport, therapeutic alliance, and therefore clinical change. Therapists should always be flexible, continue to learn about the client's particular culture, and seek consultation for support as needed.

Military

Countries around the globe sustain a wide range of armed forces stationed in far-reaching corners of the world. In 2019, the United States, Russia, and China had the strongest militaries (Global Fire Power, 2020). In the United States specifically, gambling is an all too familiar social tradition across military branches. When stationed overseas, and geographically isolated, there is lots of downtime and boredom coupled with high-stress (sometimes life-and-death) work environments. Similarly, military personnel have easy access to drugs/alcohol, tobacco, and 24/7 online gaming through accessibility on mobile phones and laptops.

In addition to more common biopsychosocial models of problem gambling, the etiology for active military may look different in terms of psychological and socio-cultural factors. For instance, military personnel may begin to bounce checks, misuse government credit cards, and engage in forgery or embezzlement. Depending on their job title and rank, military personnel may lose their rank and/or become a security risk, be forced to retire, or may receive letters of indebtedness or conduct discharges. Military personnel also appear to have high risk of suicide when compared to the general population (see also review by Kennedy *et al.*, 2005).

Military veterans, or personnel who served and no longer serve in the military, are also vulnerable to problem gambling (Newhouse, 2013) (although it is unclear if this is a chicken or egg problem—if the gambling problem started before active duty, during military service, or following service discharge). In the United States, researchers surveyed adults living in Massachusetts about their veteran status, gambling behaviors, and other demographic information. Of the adults who reported problem gambling behaviors, and reported veteran status information, 20.6% (129 gamblers from a sample of 9578) were veterans (Freeman, Volberg, & Zorn, 2019). Further, researchers have reported that gambling disorder may be higher in US female veterans when compared to male veterans, and is associated with suicide attempts in veterans who received treatment for pain within the past year (Ronzitti *et al.*, 2019). Other studies report an under-diagnosis of gambling disorder in veterans seeking mental health services in the US Veterans Affairs (VA) medical system, at six times below national estimates (Edens and Rosenheck, 2012).

Trauma and Survivor Issues

Trauma is the result of an experience or set of circumstances that is considered physically/emotionally harmful or life-threatening, that has long-lasting and adverse effects (HRSA Center for Integrated Health Solutions, 2020). Research has shown that childhood exposure and lifetime traumatic events are correlated with increased symptoms of problem gambling (Scherrer *et al.*, 2007).

Concomitantly, military veterans have high rates of trauma (e.g., post-traumatic stress disorder), and substance-use disorders including gambling (Matthieu, Wilson, & Casner, 2017). Individuals with histories of PTSD are more likely to be women and have co-occurring lifetime substance use/dependence, and are more likely to gamble as a way to cope with negative emotions (Ledgerwood & Milosevic, 2015). Further, gambling severity has been found to be correlated with frequency of PTSD symptoms (Ledgerwood & Petry, 2006). Therapist guidelines when PTSD and substance use co-occur often stress the need to treat each condition through a shared decision model to prioritize severity of behaviors/symptoms (Matthieu *et al.*, 2017), and to ensure accurate treatment (i.e., gambling as a way to deal with PTSD is a different pathway to PTSD that is independent from gambling use).

Co-Occurring Disorders

Similar to other addictions, individuals with gambling disorders are more likely to struggle with co-occurring disorders than their peers. This section gives therapists a brief overview of the complications with gambling disorder and co-occurring mental health disorders across common concerns, including psychiatric, physical (i.e., chronic illness), and socio-cultural factors.

Gambling disorder has been found to correlate with high rates of co-occurring disorders such as anxiety and depression (Barrault & Varescon, 2013), mood disorders (Lister, Milosevic, & Ledgerwood, 2015), other substance-use disorders (Cunningham-Williams *et al.*, 2000; Welte *et al.*, 2001), and attention deficit hyperactivity disorder (ADHD; Theule *et al.*, 2019). Similarly, gambling and comorbidity have also been found to be correlative with reductions in treatment adherence and higher rates of relapse (Verdejo-Garcia *et al.*, 2018). While there is much less information about comorbidity of individuals with intellectual or developmental disability and gambling disorders (see also Chapman & Wu, 2012), therapists should be aware of the potential for dual disorders between gambling and developmental disabilities (see Constantino *et al.*, 2020 for similar argument).

Individuals with co-occurring disorders are more likely to engage in gambling at a younger age, experience more severe gambling problems (Petry & Steinberg, 2005), and experience greater psychiatric symptom severity, impulsivity, and dissociation (Ledgerwood & Petry, 2006).

Another important consideration for therapists working with gamblers is the extent to which other habits or behaviors, such as gaming and Internet use, function as risk factors for gambling disorder. For instance, preliminary data has supported the association between gambling and gaming in adolescents (Wood *et al.*, 2004), while online gambling has been reported to be associated with higher prevalence of alcohol consumption and mental health disorders when compared to land-based gambling (Scholes-Balog & Hemphill, 2012; Hing *et al.*, 2017). Finally, Karlsson and colleagues (2019) recently reported a positive relationship between problem gaming and problematic Internet use with disordered gambling, even after controlling for known demographic factors such as age and gender.

Conclusion

Taken together, at-risk and problem gambling is a multifaceted disorder, characterized by situational, biopsychosocial, etiological, and idiosyncratic histories. When considering gambling as a state (in contrast to considering gambling as a trait that is therefore impossible to change), there is room for the potential to change behavioral patterns. Therapists who consider the whole person, rather than "just the gambling," will have a better understanding of the presenting symptoms and therefore subsequent treatment options.

CHAPTER 3 MODELS OF INTERVENTION

"Behavioral change is hard, but never impossible."

Treatment of any addiction is challenging. Some would argue that treating gambling disorder is much more challenging (Snippe *et al.*, 2019). A major difficulty in delivering effective treatment strategies for gambling disorders is the small percentage of gamblers who seek treatment (some reported as low as 10%; Cunningham, 2005). Individuals with gambling disorder may not seek treatment given the symptomatology of the disorder itself, the stigma and shame associated with the acknowledgment of having a gambling problem in the first place, and community or cultural stigma of gambling disorders generally (see also Suurvali *et al.*, 2009). Of those who actively seek treatment, it has been estimated that up to half will drop out by the second session (Ladouceur, Grosselin, *et al.*, 2001; Ladouceur *et al.*, 2009).

As a general rule of thumb, when determining what intervention strategies to use, most evidence-based practice guidelines focus on the quality of scientific design employed, the replication of findings across multiple independent research teams and/or centers, and implementation practicality and applicability. However, given the limited empirical evidence on the long-term effectiveness of known therapeutic approaches (Cowlishaw *et al.*, 2012), is it "impossible to define 'best practice' treatment standards for addressing disordered gambling at this time" (Snippe *et al.*, 2019, p.196).

Given the aforementioned barriers and current state of the literature base, the current chapter will focus on a person-in-environment approach to clinical practice and therapeutic intervention (e.g., Greene, 2008; Wilson & Matthieu, 2015). In this way, the chapter will provide therapists with an overall understanding of the various types of theoretical considerations for treatment success (i.e., stages of change), treatment approaches and strategies that have been empirically validated, treatment delivery considerations, and mechanisms of change within treatment approaches and delivery modalities, with a lens towards tailoring outcomes and treatment goals across diverse populations of gamblers (Gonzalez-Ibanez, Rosel, & Moreno, 2005). In this way, therapists should consider 1) the client, 2) the setting, and 3) the current skill set of therapeutic styles, models, and strategies discussed. With this goal in mind, the current chapter seeks to help therapists establish a working knowledge of various intervention strategies and models, with the actual "how to do the strategy in treatment" in Chapter 4: Models of Intervention—Applied.

Transtheoretical Model

Before diving into the models of intervention for gambling disorder, it is important to discuss client motivation not only to seek treatment but to seek (and maintain) abstinence. Motivation, as a construct, is considered a person's state that is influential towards engaging in new behaviors (i.e., alternatives to gambling) or old patterns of behaviors (i.e., gambling and related behaviors). The transtheoretical model of behavioral change (TTM; Prochaska and Velicer, 1997) offers a six-stage model to understand, and subsequently influence, motivational change. The six stages are precontemplation, contemplation, preparation, action, maintenance, and termination. While discussion of this model often suggests that it functions in a linear way (as in first clients must experience precontemplation, before experiencing contemplation, then preparation, etc.), actual motivation and subsequent action to change does not always or necessarily proceed in this way. Rather, individuals may be in certain stages for specific habits or behaviors, and in other stages for other habits or behaviors. Each person will come to therapy at different stages of change, and progression through each stage isn't necessarily a linear process (see also Wohl & Sztainert, 2011).

Precontemplation occurs when the client has not yet acknowledged a problem behavior to be changed and is often referred to as "denial" or "lack of responsibility for actions." The *contemplation* stage occurs when the person acknowledges a problem but is still unsure or not ready to fully commit to change. Clients in this stage usually need assistance with figuring out what life looks like without gambling and weighing pros and cons of continued gambling or stopped gambling (see also Chapter 4: Models of Intervention—Applied on how to conduct similar exercises).

The *preparation* or determination stage occurs when the client is ready to commit to making change. Clients in this stage are ready for therapists to assist with creating a plan for not gambling or reducing gambling. What do the days of the week (workdays and weekends) look like? What will the client do to combat boredom? What will the client tell friends and family? What alternative resources can/will the client use? Where are local GA meetings, and when do they meet? Are there online meetings the client can attend? What financial restitution plan will the client use? How will they access money (i.e., prepare by ordering a prepaid Visa card and connecting to the bank)?

The *action* stage occurs when the client not only believes they can change but are actively involved in engaging in new/alternative behaviors rather than old patterns of behavior. Engagement in this stage is dynamic, and clients will vary in terms of how successful they are in staying within this stage. Therapists can assist clients in this stage with applying behavioral exercises and "to-dos" to help the client stay active in engaging in new patterns of behavior, including identifying alternative activities (e.g., journaling, reading, exercise/taking walks, meditation, etc.), connecting with friends and family for accountability, participation in self-exclusion, etc. Finally, the *maintenance and termination* stage occurs when the person is successful in avoiding relapse to old patterns of behavior, lasting anywhere from six months to five years or longer. During this stage, therapists can help clients with staying aware of relapse warning signs and other issues that could serve to trigger relapse (e.g., friendships/

relationships, romance issues such as infidelity or death of a loved one, work/employment pursuits or failures, etc.).

Treatment Approaches and Stance of Therapy

Cognitive Therapy

Cognition has long been of interest to philosophers, psychologists, and others interested in human behavior. Cognition can be defined as thoughts or thought patterns that encompass symbolic relations between knowledge and understanding by way of experience (e.g., thought, taste, touch, smell). In this way, cognitive therapy focuses on thinking patterns that are distorted, faulty, or otherwise maladaptive for the client (e.g., Fortune & Goodie, 2012).

Early work using cognitive therapy (e.g., Ladouceur *et al.*, 1998) targeted cognitive distortions, erroneous thoughts and beliefs about gambling, and negative thoughts to reduce cognitive biases triggered by environmental stimuli that elicit gambling behaviors (i.e., addiction cues such as images, sounds, or smells that are part of the game when gambling). Common erroneous thought patterns include illusions of control (where gamblers believe they can somehow control if they win or not), gambler's fallacy (false beliefs about probabilities), and other rigid and superstitious rules about gambling. Research on cognitive therapy with problem gambling has been shown to be more efficacious than no-treatment control in individual sessions (Ladouceur *et al.*, 2001) and group therapy format (Ladouceur *et al.*, 2003).

Behavior Therapy

Behavior therapies focus on reducing occurrences of specific target behaviors (usually considered maladaptive or unwanted) and increasing occurrences of new alternative (more adaptive) behaviors and behavioral patterns. Common behavioral strategies include systematic and imaginal desensitization, identification of functional relationships between environment and target behavior(s), and contingency management (see also Petry, 2005). Imaginal desensitization, for example, involves allowing the client to visualize aspects related to gambling, including thoughts and urges, while visualizing themselves stopping and exiting the venue, or refraining from gambling (e.g., Whiting & Dixon, 2013; Grant *et al.*, 2011). Contingency management (CM) involves providing reinforcement (i.e., prize or voucher for money or similar) to clients who abstain from behavioral patterns. CM has been shown to be incredibly efficacious in the treatment of substance-use disorders (Prendergast *et al.*, 2006), and has been shown not to increase gambling behaviors (Petry *et al.*, 2006). Despite this, only two studies have been conducted to date using contingency management as a treatment for problem gambling (e.g., West, 2008; Christensen *et al.*, 2018; see also Petry, 2010 for discussion on controversies and challenges with using CM).

Cognitive-Behavioral Therapy

Cognitive-behavioral therapies (CBT) represent a combination of both cognitive approaches and behavioral strategies. The goal of CBT for gambling treatment is to target cognitive distortions and related erroneous belief systems that are associated with gambling (Fong, 2005). Research to date has shown effective outcomes of CBT with adult (Petry, 2005) and adolescent gamblers (Ladouceur, Boisvert, & Dumont, 1994), and CBT has been shown to be effective in both individual and group settings. For instance, Oei, Raylu, and Casey (2010) randomized gamblers into one of three groups: individual CBT (two-hour weekly sessions for six weeks), group CBT (two half-hour sessions for six weeks), or waitlist control (no treatment). At the end of treatment and at a six-month follow-up, gambling rates in both treatment conditions significantly reduced when compared to the control group.

Recently, the Brief Escape and Action Treatment program (BEAT Gambling Program; Stewart *et al.*, 2016) was created to target two types of gamblers: action vs. escape gamblers (or Pathways 1 with or without emotional and biological vulnerabilities). Within the BEAT program, gamblers are taught:

> to identify and challenge unique thinking errors and to engage in distinct behavioral strategies as means of overcoming problem gambling. For example, escape gamblers are trained in more adaptive

means of relieving distress; whereas action gamblers are trained in less risky means of achieving excitement and stimulation. (Snippe *et al.*, 2019, p.216)

CBT has also been shown to be adaptable to fit special populations, including those impacted with co-occurring disorders (Champine & Petry, 2010) and traumatic brain injuries (Guercio, Johnson, & Dixon, 2012). CBT is also easily adaptable to fit a client's cultural affiliation/background (e.g., Okuda *et al.*, 2009). For example, challenging a client's beliefs about number interpretations may not be consistent with working with diverse communities or cultures, and doing so could minimize the cultural norms of the client's family or heritage. Within treatment, using behavioral techniques (rather than relying solely on challenging cognitive distortions) is useful to help clients with problem-solving how to engage in new patterns of behavior rather than old patterns of behavior (Okuda *et al.*, 2009). Therapists can help clients identify risky situations that could potentially expose them to gambling, by *"closing all the doors"* that lead to gambling. Consider working with clients to delete apps on a smartphone that can access any form of betting or gambling, canceling credit cards, changing passwords on online accounts, and setting up automatic deposit of their paycheck into a bank account without direct access, in order to assist gamblers with engaging in new patterns of behaviors. Similarly, self-exclusion has been shown to be an effective behavioral intervention for motivated gamblers (Ladouceur *et al.*, 2000).

While promising, it is important to highlight that CBT has been cautiously recommended as the "gold standard" for gambling treatment (Rickwood *et al.*, 2010), as the empirical support of CBT may not necessarily generalize to all types of gamblers (see also Cowlishaw *et al.*, 2012; Westphal, 2008 for similar warnings). However, while isolating effective treatment components may not always be feasible, three primary areas of research have been found to be effective in treating disordered gambling (which are included in most applications of CBT and third-wave behavior therapies discussed below). *Imaginal desensitization*, a variation of systematic desensitization, has been shown to help reduce physiological arousal and hyperactivation towards gambling stimuli; *in-vivo exposure with response prevention and control of stimuli* has been shown to decrease cravings and urges to gamble while active participation in replacement behaviors in the presence of gambling stimuli; and *cognitive restructuring* has been shown to effectively alter distorted thoughts (see also Echeburúa, Fernández-Montalvo, & Báez, 2000).

Third-Wave Behavior Therapy

Behavior therapy has been commonly associated with an evolution of "waves"; from the original behavioral modification in the 1950s and 1960s, to the cognitive-behavioral revolution beginning in the 1970s (Kendall & Hollon, 1979), to the Eastern influence of mindfulness- and acceptance-based philosophies of today's "third wave" (see also Hayes, 2004). Third-wave (or third-generation) behavior therapies focus on broadening the client's behavior patterns over the reduction and elimination of symptoms, to emphasize the persistence towards new repertoires rather than reduce or suppress triggers or symptoms that result in engagement in old behavioral patterns. These interventions have focused on non-judgmental attitudes and acceptance of all things (events, people, feelings, urges, etc.) to the present moment.

One concept that is similar across third-wave approaches is that of experiential avoidance (EA), or the overarching behavioral pattern that is the result of experiences where an individual is unwilling to confront aversive or painful private events (i.e., thoughts, memories, urges/cravings; experiences that occur internally), and, in turn, engage in behaviors that reduce "frequency or form of these events, such as disassociation escape, and avoidance" (Riley, 2014, p.164). Third-wave behavior therapies target EA through a range of techniques, unique and yet similar across modalities. Examples of third-wave therapies include mindfulness-based relapse prevention (MBRP; Bowen, Chawla, & Marlatt, 2010), mindfulness-based cognitive therapy (MBCT; Segal, Williams, & Teasdale, 2002), acceptance and commitment therapy (ACT; Dixon & Wilson, 2014), and dialectical behavior therapy (DBT; Christensen *et al.*, 2013).

Mindfulness, for instance, has been developed as a stand-alone treatment modality (e.g., Griffiths, Shonin, & Van Gordon, 2016) and as a component within other forms of behavior therapies (such as mindfulness-based relapse prevention; Witkiewitz *et al.*, 2014; and acceptance and commitment therapy; Hayes, Strosahl, & Wilson, 1999/2011). Techniques used throughout mindfulness-based intervention strategies often include awareness, visualization, and present-moment focus. Research to date has shown mindfulness-based interventions have increased positive coping strategies towards urges (Toneatto, Vettese, & Nguyen, 2007), increased tolerance of negative physiological experiences (Bowen *et al.*, 2009), and decreased preference for structural characteristics that are disadvantageous (i.e., near-miss outcomes or losses disguised as wins; Nastally & Dixon, 2012). Further, in a recent meta-analysis, Maynard and colleagues (2018) found seven articles that empirically tested a mindfulness-based intervention with problematic or disordered gamblers. Of the studies identified, mindfulness-based interventions were found to have positive and significant effects on gambling symptoms/behaviors, urges, and financial outcomes (Maynard *et al.*, 2018).

Similarly, some therapeutic models infuse mindfulness and acceptance--based intervention strategies into overarching models. For instance, mindfulness-based cognitive therapy (MBCT) emphasizes mindfulness-meditation practices to promote awareness of the present moment, in addition to dismantling and responding to negative thoughts or feelings (Segal *et al.*, 2002). To date, MBCT has been shown to be effective at reducing gambling behavior in single-case studies (i.e., de Lisle, Dowling, & Sabura Allen, 2011), and, in a controlled study, has been shown to reduce gambling severity, gambling urges, and co-occurring psychiatric symptoms at the end of treatment and at three-month follow up when compared to gamblers in a waitlist control (Toneatto, Pillai, & Courtice, 2014). Similarly, acceptance and commitment therapy (ACT; Hayes *et al.*, 1999) emphasizes contacting the present moment, open non-judgmental awareness and acceptance of aversive and pleasurable events or experiences and engaging in behaviors that are consistent with one's value systems. While research on ACT with problem gamblers is still in early days, preliminary evidence has shown differences in brain activation patterns between winning outcomes and losing outcomes when compared to control participants (Dixon, Wilson, & Habib, 2016), and changes in preferences towards structural features of gambling like near-miss outcomes (Nastally & Dixon, 2012).

Motivational Interviewing

Motivational interviewing (MI; Rollnick & Miller, 1995) is considered a style of counselling rather than a treatment modality *per se*, and centers around how a therapist can use constructive conversation about behavioral change to understand "the client's perspective and minimize resistance... Strategies and techniques are used to explore the [client's] values and goals and their relation to the addictive problem, and to elicit motivation for change from the client" (Rollnick & Allison, 2004, pp.106–107). MI focuses on the client's motivational state, or readiness to change, and relies on identifying the client's readiness, ambivalence, and resistance (Rollnick & Miller, 1995). Client *readiness* to change is the extent to which the client's perspective and beliefs about change are congruent with behaviors engaged in—essentially, how much of *what the client says* matches up with *what the client does* (Rollnick & Allison, 2004). *Ambivalence* is often considered a central concept within MI and refers to the extent to which the client expresses mixed feelings or contradictions between stated values (i.e., "I want to quit gambling") and behaviors engaged in (i.e., continued gambling). It is important for therapists to remember that change is a process, marked by some degree of ambivalence, as change is not made without inconvenience; it is therefore important for therapists to consider the inconvenience from the perspective of the client and the client's goals and core values (Rollnick & Allison, 2004). Finally, *resistance* is considered as a general reluctance to change, opposition to other people's (therapist, client friends/family, society, etc.) value systems.

Common principles used in MI adhere to person-centered therapeutic stances, including expressing empathy and empathic listening, rolling with resistance, and creating a safe place for clients to determine how specific target behavior might not align with their value systems, while supporting client self-efficacy (Miller & Rollnick, 2012; Rollnick & Allison, 2004). Taking into account the core philosophical stance of MI, researchers have argued that MI may be an effective treatment for gambling disorder, given the deficit or impairment of motivation and control that is commonplace within disordered gambling, in addition to the number of gamblers who recover naturally or without professional treatment (e.g., Hodgins & Diskin, 2008).

Meta-analyses on the effects of MI in treating disordered gambling have yielded promising results. Yakovenko and colleagues (2015) identified five articles where a total of 477 problem gamblers were subjected to MI or waitlist control. Dependent variables included days gambled per month and dollars lost per month. Results of the metal analyses found that gamblers assigned to MI interventions on average significantly reduced dollars spent gambling compared to controls up to three months following treatment (Yakovenko *et al.*, 2015). Further, when MI is added to other more commonly researched treatment modalities (i.e., CBT), treatment effects have also been positive. For instance, MI-enhanced CBT has been shown to result in significant gambling reduction following treatment when compared to gamblers in control conditions such as GA referral (Grant *et al.*, 2009). Further, Petry and colleagues (2008) investigated the effects of four treatment options for problem gamblers: 1) assessment only, 2) ten minutes of brief advice about gambling, 3) single MI session, or 4) MI session plus three CBT sessions. Following intervention, brief advice was the only group that decreased gambling behavior following six-week and nine-month follow-ups, even though no significant differences were found between the three interventions (suggesting that some treatment is better than no treatment). Interestingly, attrition rates were highest in the "MI plus three CBT sessions" group, with only 33% of participants assigned to this group completing all four sessions (Petry *et al.*, 2008).

Pharmacological Therapy

A biomedical approach to problem and disordered gambling includes pharmacological therapies, with or without psychotherapy. Currently, as of this writing, there is no approved pharmacological treatment (i.e., drug) approved by any of the world's top approval agencies (i.e., Food and Drug Administration (FDA; USA), European Medicines Agency (EMA), Medicines and Healthcare Regulatory Agency in the UK). However, research has been investigating pharmacological therapies, with primary evidence on paroxetine glutamatergic compounds and opioid antagonists (i.e., naltrexone). Antidepressants, mood stabilizers, and antipsychotic treatments, however, have been shown to be ineffective for decreasing gambling in the absence of comorbid psychiatric disorders (Achab & Khazaal, 2011).

Opioid antagonists, such as naloxone and naltrexone, have been approved by the Food and Drug Administration (FDA; USA) for treatment of alcohol use and opioid disorders (Theriot & Azadfard, 2019). However, emerging research has found opioid antagonists, including naltrexone, are effective as daily prescription or as targeted medication consumed during risky situations when relapse is likely to occur (Lahti *et al.*, 2010). Similarly, six months of naltrexone has been shown to impact gambling abstinence up to six months following treatment (Van den Brink, 2012). While promising, the combination of both psychotherapy and pharmacotherapy may provide better rates of client retention than therapy or drug treatment alone (see Kraus, Etuk, & Potenza, 2020).

Treatment Considerations: Modality, Duration, and Targeting Relapse

When conducting treatment, therapists are typically comfortable with considering and selecting what treatment approach to use with a specific client. However, other aspects such as treatment modality (i.e., online, face-to-face, technology-driven sessions, etc.), duration (i.e., length of session vs. length of treatment), and treatment targets (i.e., targeting gambling behaviors, alternative behaviors, and explicitly targeting and treating relapse) may be more convoluted and challenging to discern. The following section seeks to provide therapists with a brief overview of these considerations when working with problem gamblers.

Online Modalities

In today's world, like everything else we can access online or via the Internet, so too can we access (and therefore provide) mental health services or therapy. Online treatment modalities have surged with recent advancements and accessibility of technology and the Internet, and have shown promise as an option for gamblers unsure about seeking treatment (Canale *et al.*, 2016). Additionally, the use of technology within face-to-face sessions, including smartphones and applications, have been shown to be an effective tool for assisting clients with completing homework between sessions (Magnusson *et al.*, 2019).

Research on online treatment modalities has taken a two-pronged approach to understanding the efficacy of treatment delivery: applying known treatments via technological delivery formats with and without a "live" therapist. Cognitive behavior therapy, for instance, has been tailored to an online format, and has been found to lower problem gambling symptoms and levels of depression and anxiety in concerned significant others (Nilsson *et al.*, 2017). Similarly, Luquiens and colleagues (2015) conducted a randomized control trial with 1122 non-therapy-seeking online problem poker players. Gamblers were randomly assigned to one of three groups: 1) personalized normalized feedback on gambling status by email, 2) a downloadable self-help book adapted from the six-step CBT program by Ladouceur and Lachance (Ladouceur & Lachance, 2007) with no guidance, and 3) the same CBT program emailed weekly by a trained psychologist with personalized guidance. Following six weeks of treatment, researchers reported no significant differences in problem gambling severity across the groups. Interestingly, however, high attrition rates were reported in the group receiving CBT with emailed guidance from a psychologist. These results suggest that non-treatment-seeking gamblers may not have motivation to change their behavior, and therefore any treatment will be ineffective at producing behavioral change.

Furthermore, motivational interviewing has been used in an online treatment modality. Hodgins and colleagues (2009) assigned 314 gamblers to one of four groups: 1) brief motivational treatment of telephone interview and mailed self-help workbook; 2) brief motivational booster treatment (telephone interview, mailed self-help workbook, and six booster telephone calls over nine-month period); 3) mailed self-help workbook only; and 4) six-week waitlist control. Following intervention, gamblers assigned to both MI interventions reported a decrease in gambling frequency at six weeks and six months of follow-up when compared to gamblers assigned to the control groups. However, gamblers in the brief booster MI treatment did not show greater improvements when compared to gamblers in brief MI alone (Hodgins *et al.*, 2009, p.950).

Brief Treatment

In addition to treatment delivery modality, the duration or length of treatment has also been of interest to researchers. Given the high dropout rates of problem gamblers who seek therapy, it is important to consider brief forms of treatment, to ensure an adequate effect of a small dose of treatment. Brief treatments typically last between ten minutes and four hours and can be a cost-effective alternative for clients with diminished gambling severity (Petry et al., 2008).

Brief interventions have been found to be more effective than no treatment at all, both with adult problem gamblers (Petry et al., 2008) and college student gamblers (Petry et al., 2009). Similarly, brief interventions have been explored with motivational interviewing (Petry et al., 2008, 2009), cognitive-behavioral therapy (Petry, 2005), and acceptance and commitment therapy (Nastally & Dixon, 2012). Interestingly, brief interventions have been found to be equally effective regardless of treatment used, as shown by equal decreases in gambling severity of college gamblers following brief MI and brief CBT (Larimer et al., 2012).

Relapse Prevention

From a behavioral perspective, relapse occurs when both new behavioral patterns and old behavioral patterns (i.e., stealing or lying to obtain cash to place a bet) fail to access adequate reinforcers; as a result, gambling relapse occurs as a way for the individual to escape/avoid life stressors and/or access action-oriented experiences. Relapse not only impacts the individual or client, but can also impact familial and romantic relationships, which in turn can serve as triggers for continued or persistent gambling.

Relapse prevention models (Marlatt & Gordon, 1985) consider the various pathways to recovery processes generally speaking, to apply them with a client in therapy to target and potentially reduce rates of relapse. Relapse prevention focuses on targeting risk factors or triggers for gambling use, and working with clients to determine where potential risk for relapse is high, to identify alternative solutions to those conditions/periods when relapse is likely (Chambless & Ollendick, 2001). Said another way, therapists work with clients to develop a plan for "*closing the doors*" that have potential to lead to relapse. When relapse is considered as part of the symptomatology of the disorder itself (rather than as a "weakness" of the client), therapists can work with clients on recognizing warning signs of potential relapse, and preparing for what to do instead of relapse.

Relapse prevention has been found to result in higher rates of abstinence from gambling up to 12-month follow-up in both group and individual treatment modalities (Echeburúa *et al.*, 2000). Similarly, relapse prevention models have been established (i.e., mindfulness-based relapse prevention) and have been shown to have effective outcomes in reducing gambling symptomatology (O'Neill, 2017). However, meta-analyses conducted on mindfulness-based relapse prevention (MBRP) for substance-use disorders have not found significant differences that favor MBRP (Grant *et al.*, 2017).

Conclusion

Research on effective treatment approaches for gambling disorder have found behavioral (i.e., imaginal desensitization, stimulus control, exposure) and cognitive (i.e., cognitive restructuring) techniques to produce positive outcomes across gambling measures. However, while research has found useful techniques and applications with problem gamblers, therapists are still cautioned on the lack of "best practice" treatment standards for disordered gambling (see also Snippe *et al.*, 2019). When therapists consider which treatment approaches to use, there is a clear positive relationship between person-in-environment approaches and decreased maladaptive symptomatology (i.e., Wilson & Matthieu, 2015). To this end, therapists should consider the client's position/perspective in "stages of change," to help guide where to start treatment. As discussed, different therapeutic strategies are needed for clients in precontemplation compared to when clients are in action stages. Further, therapists should also consider infusing relapse prevention efforts, particularly when clients are in the action stage and during periods of abstinence.

CHAPTER 4 MODELS OF INTERVENTION— APPLIED

"Success is a lived experience, quantified by the number of times you get back up after you fall down."

Clinical intervention strategies, as discussed in Chapter 3: Models of Intervention, provide a range of therapeutic tools and choices for working with a diverse array of clients. In today's world, most therapists are familiar with the phrase "evidence-based practice" or the more recent "evidence-informed practice." Both approaches focus on ensuring therapists use intervention programs/models that are backed and supported by science. Often, this requires therapists to stay updated with current clinical research trends and completion of continuing education hours.

When determining what intervention strategies to use, most evidence-based practice (EBP) guidelines focus on quality of scientific design, replication of findings across multiple independent research centers and/or research teams, and implementation practicality and applicability. While some modalities have been more researched than others (e.g., cognitive-behavioral therapy; Petry, 2005), therapists decide what intervention or therapeutic approach to use based on a myriad of factors, from feasibility and confidence of implementing to costs of further supervision/training/implementation, and fitness for client needs. From an EBP perspective, when selecting an intervention strategy, therapists are expected to follow a process based on the client's condition and needs of care: 1) ask about clinical goals/outcomes of therapy; 2) acquire relevant literature (to determine evidence-supported measurements/assessments, therapeutic strategies/techniques, etc.); 3) conduct literature appraisal (i.e., questioning any research to ensure the study is valid, results are meaningful and pertain to client); 4) apply the evidence with the client; and 5) assess and evaluate the success of the selected treatment (see also Portney, 2020). While EBP has been suggested for use in all aspects of clinical practice (e.g., Kitson, Harvey, & McCormack, 1998), evidence-informed clinical practice (Nevo & Slonim-Nevo, 2011) is more realistic for all therapists to abide by.

One question frequently debated by researchers, therapists, and policy analysts alike is the dose of treatment needed for "success" to occur. In other words, how many sessions of what type of intervention strategy (e.g., cognitive-behavioral therapy, motivational interviewing, contingency management, etc.) are needed for the "most" gamblers to stop or abstain from harmful use (to include abstinence)? A recent meta-analysis on the dose effects of face-to-face gambling psychotherapy treatments found a positive association between the intended treatment dose and received treatment dose (i.e., number of sessions) and magnitude of treatment outcome following treatment, suggesting the more treatment sessions the larger treatment outcome potential (Pfund *et al.*, 2020).

As such, the current chapter will highlight how to infuse evidence-informed clinical practice into treatment for problem and disordered gamblers. However, instead of targeting each specific intervention approach or treatment model (as described in Chapter 3: Models of Intervention), the current chapter will focus on walking the reader through how to use effective treatment strategies with gambling clients. To this end, the chapter will highlight 1) how to "close the doors" for clients, 2) how to address pathways consideration (i.e., access and availability factors, chasing, biological/emotional vulnerabilities, etc.) in session, and 3) therapeutic considerations when treating gamblers (i.e., relapse prevention, when to walk away/terminate relationship, session structure/format, etc.).

In the beginning of gambling treatment, like other mental health disorders, therapists must start with assessment: information gathering about the who, what, when, where, why, and how. This aspect to treatment is discussed in depth in Chapter 5: Where to Start and What to Ask, and is mentioned here to highlight the first aspect of treatment needed when conducting evidence-informed clinical practice. Further, identifying the conditions that are more likely to result in gambling will provide helpful information to use during treatments described below.

Closing the Doors

In the first few sessions of treatment, the therapist should assess for gambling symptomatology, gambling pathway (i.e., behaviorally conditioned gambler vs. emotionally and biologically vulnerable conditioned gambler vs. impulsive/antisocial conditioned gambler), co-occurring mental health disorders (if any), and conditions that make it more likely the client will gamble. One of the most important "asks" for the client, after the aforementioned factors, is to discover all the "doors" the client uses to gamble.

When first discussing the concept of "doors" with the client, it is important to start with providing education to clients on the doors of their gambling early on in treatment. Help clients think about people, places, and things that influence their gambling. For instance, who are the people they gamble with? Where do they gamble? Is there something about the calendar year that results in more/less gambling (e.g., sports season may be a trigger for gambling, or the anniversary of a big win or the death of loved one may also be a trigger for gambling). Client demographic and "life" factors to consider as potential doors include financial factors (such as large debts, access to cash, "family money," etc.), age (including age of first gambling experience and current age), history of trauma or power/control issues, relationship status (i.e., single vs. married vs. divorced), and access to and availability of gambling (including apps on phone, location of gambling arena/venue, patterns of use, etc.).

Ways to close recognized doors will vary, but can include deleting apps on the phone, voluntarily participating in self-exclusion, downloading blocking software on all technology devices, etc. The goal is to find all doors that, when opened or available, the client walks through the door and causes damage (i.e., walking through the door results in gambling, which in turn causes further negative outcomes or consequences in the client's life). In this way, therapists work with clients to identify short-term behaviors and strategies the client can implement to "close the doors," as a means to help clients visualize a different way to approach the same sets of issues they use gambling to deal with.

Later in treatment, begin to look into more nuanced and "harder to see" doors. For instance, are there personal relationships that impact a client's gambling use/misuse? Are there different activities the client can be (or wants to be) engaged in? Are there familial or friendships that may trigger gambling use? How does the client interact with family/friends at events or celebrations? Do friends and family know about gambling problems? How does the client avoid triggering events while still having meaningful relationships?

For some clients, considering the stages of change can be helpful to determining what doors are open and/or hidden from clients. What stage of change is the client in? Consider using a "stages of change" handout and applying it to all habits exhibited by the client, to discern if or how gambling is similar to other behaviors or habits exhibited by the client. Are the doors for gambling similar to the doors for other habits? Given the high dropout rates of gamblers in treatment, it is crucial to use motivational interviewing language and approach during treatment, to ensure the therapist 1) meets the client at the stage they are in, and 2) validates while supporting change of the client.

One example useful for clients in the precontemplation, contemplation, or planning stages of change is the "Pro and Cons Grid for Gambling." Clients are asked to list pros and cons to giving up gambling as well as continuing gambling. Answers are then used to identify barriers and factors that get in the way of the client moving into action and refraining from gambling. When discussing answers with the client, it is important to spend moderate time on answers to "Continuing to Gamble—Pros" and spend the majority of time going over answers to "Continuing to Gamble—Cons."

Table 4.1 includes client responses to this exercise over the years; these are provided as examples for therapists rather than as an example to be considered from a single person. When working with clients, we have noticed it is easiest for most to complete the cons of continued gambling and the pros of stopping than the other boxes. Sometimes, clients will try to make answers the same across sections (e.g., con for continued gambling is family isn't supportive, so pro to stopping gambling is family will be supportive); other times, clients will create opposites (e.g., con for continued gambling is the family is angry, so pro to stopping gambling is my family will be happy with me; con for continued gambling is I have no money, so pro to stopping gambling is I'll be out of debt). Some clients may struggle to find the words, and will say there are no pros in gambling (even though we all know there are, or they wouldn't be doing it!). A big concern for most clients is the fear of when they relapse, with most clients including "I could relapse" under cons of stopping gambling.

Table 4.1 Client Example of Pros and Cons Grid for Gambling

Client answers are represented in italics, and therapist considerations are represented by *.

	Pros	Cons
Continued Gambling	• *Excitement* • *Opportunity to make money* • *It's fun* • *Gives me something to do; I'm good at it* • *Still can avoid situations or problems* *Struggles to be honest with what gambling really does for them	• *My family is angry, practically hates me* • *I'm in more debt all the time* • *I feel depressed after gambling; not happy anymore* • *I keep lying to people* • *Spouse will leave me* *Easily lists immediate consequences *Often aligns with others' expectations/desires
Stop Gambling	• *My family is more supportive* • *I'll have more money* • *I'll sleep better* • *I won't have to keep lying* *Immediately lists benefits of what other people want from them to stop	• *What will I do with my time?* • *All my friends gamble too* • *How will I distract myself when I'm overwhelmed?* • *I'll have to be around family more* • *I'll have to be responsible and accountable* • *What if I can't stay stopped and I relapse?* *When client struggles to complete this square, still in contemplative stage of change

When doing this exercise, it is imperative for therapists to take a non-judgmental approach, and to meet the client where they are with filling out the matrix. If clients say "there are no pros in gambling," therapists should compassionately probe for different factors that occur before, during, or after gambling, to help the client contact and articulate their experiences of the pros/cons of gambling and those of stopping gambling. Clients should be provided with the space and permission to be honest when doing the exercise.

Addressing Gambling Symptoms

Cognitive Distortions

As discussed in Chapter 2: Understanding Gambling Disorder, cognitive distortions are a common symptom of gambling disorder. Distorted thinking is not a "door" to be closed, as it keeps showing back up (and therefore isn't something that can be closed). Instead, cognitive distortions need continued attention and rehearsal/practice with reframing thoughts about gambling. While some therapists may feel an urgency to address cognitive distortions immediately at the beginning of treatment, we would instead recommend therapists consider waiting to challenge distorted thinking until mid-treatment, once a relationship has developed between therapist and client.

Techniques useful in challenging distorted thinking range from informal (i.e., having discussions where the therapist challenges client thoughts and distortions) to more formalized exercises. For instance, when clients make commitments that they do not follow through with, challenging their thought processes may help them to contact what they *actually do* rather than what their thoughts *say about what will/did happen*. Furthermore, exposure to information regarding aspects of gambling, including the independence of turns, can influence gambling motivation and perception about the game of chance itself (e.g., Benhsain, Taillefer, & Ladouceur, 2004). Interventions of this sort have been argued as a crucial intervention strategy, accounting for treatment gains in 85% of patients (Ladouceur *et al.*, 2001) in both individual (Ladouceur *et al.*, 2001; Benhsain *et al.*, 2004) and group treatment settings (Ladouceur *et al.*, 2003),

One such intervention strategy focused on the notion of randomness and the independence of turns is the *Coin Toss* (derived from Ladouceur *et al.*, 2002). During the Coin Toss exercise, the therapist starts by taking out a piece of paper and numbering 1–10. The therapist gives the client a coin and has them flip the coin while the therapist writes if it landed on heads or tails. The therapist only allows the client to toss the coin nine times. During these trials, the client may be sharing distorted thoughts or beliefs such as "look at all those heads!" or "the next one has to be tails because X." After the ninth toss, the therapist may ask what the client thinks the last toss will be, but may not allow the client to actually toss the coin. Instead, the therapist talks with the client about new cognitive distortions that emerge when old ones are not reinforced by the event itself (i.e., the coin toss). To put it another way, by not allowing for the final tenth toss, the therapist withholds the possibility to reinforce the faulty belief/thought because the outcome never occurs.

By reinforcing the alternative, namely the independence of turns between each of the nine toss events, therapists can use the coin toss example as a way to help the client shift preferences and attitudes towards gambling-related thoughts/beliefs. It is important for clients to understand that the history of events no longer is relevant in the discussion of independence of turns; the thought that "the next toss must be X" is false, even if the outcome is in actuality X. Therapists should consider asking the client about how similar cognitive distortions emerge in aspects of their gambling activities. How do similar experiences show up for them, before, during, or after gambling or other life experiences?

Habituation

Identifying patterns of habituation within the client's life and particularly related to gambling is a central component to successful treatment. To assist the client with identifying patterns of gambling use, it is important to *identify when and why the client gambles*. Is it always on a Friday night (and when probed further, you discover the client is single and all alone on weekends)? Is it always late at night (and when probed further, you discover the client works 14+-hour days, and uses gambling as a way to wind down after work)? Is it a case of the "fuck its" (and when probed further, you discover client gets cases of *fuck it* whenever life gets too stressful, or when they don't feel as if they have a way out)? Therapists should also consider directly asking about client perspectives on self-care (for clients who don't know how to do self-care, gambling may be considered part of their self-care routine) and power/control dynamics. When clients feel they don't have control, do they gamble as a way to say "I'll show you"? For some clients, gambling can be a way to regain control, particularly if they feel as if they have little to no control in other aspects of their life, such as relationships, jobs, children, etc.

While there are a variety of ways therapists can address habitation in session, we will highlight a few examples here. One of the more effective ways to assist clients with identifying habitation and influencing behavioral change is to reduce the client's gambling into a series of decision points from the thoughts about gambling to the actual gambling event. The goal of the exercise *Decision Points* is to identify various time points within a larger chain of events that clients can then attend to and actively decide to choose to engage in an alternative behavior. To put it a different way, this exercise assists clients to get out of habitation, as it requires active responding in the presence of triggering environmental stimuli/events. For example, people often report in therapy that they get in their car after a long shift, and because they get into the car they are "destined" to gamble. Clients also report "blacking out," stating they recall getting into their car, and then "waking up" in the casino, playing their machine. These reports suggest a habituation effect, wherein clients no longer engage in active decision making. The goal, then, is to break down decision points for every step in the chain between getting into the car and gambling in the casino. To illustrate this point, we've broken down all the steps Client X engages in before a gambling episode (Box 4.1).

To take this exercise one step further, particularly for clients who are unable to generalize the exercise from the session to real life (i.e., clients who are unable to put this into practice between sessions), therapists can consider having the client record themselves on their smartphone or mobile device, talking about all the decision points and specific behaviors to engage in to get from work to home without stopping to gamble. Clients can play the recording on their phone, in their car, over and over again until they reach home, successfully, without stopping to gamble.

Box 4.1 Overview of the decision points Client X has from getting into the car (decision 1) to placing a bet (decision 23)

1. Get into car	13. Turn off car
2. Turn car on	14. Unbuckle seat belt
3. Buckle seat belt	15. Open car door
4. Get car out of park, into drive	16. Step out of car
5. Drive to end of parking lot	17. Close car door
6. Make left, get onto highway	18. Lock the car
7. Get off highway at exit	19. Walk to door of casino
8. Go left at first light	20. Walk through door of casino
9. Go right at next light	21. Get cash, find game/machine
10. Enter casino parking lot	22. Sit down
11. Find parking spot	23. Place bet
12. Park the car	

Another way to address habituation is through mindfulness-based intervention strategies. *Mindfulness* can be useful to assist the client with contacting the present moment, which is typically what clients avoid before/during/after a gambling episode. When clients struggle with contacting the various decision points throughout the chain of events that result in gambling, using mindfulness and visualization processes can be helpful. For instance, meditation exercises that help the client practice contacting the present moment may be a helpful first step towards getting clients to remain in the present, particularly during triggering experiences. Asking the client to visualize themselves gambling, and walking away from the game or engaging in an alternative response at step 5 or 10, can assist the client to visualize themselves engaging in the alternative behaviors (which in turn may increase the likelihood that they engage in those alternative behaviors the next time they experience step 5 or 10).

Finally, for clients stuck in ambivalence, exercises that force clients to experience their ambivalence in different ways may also be helpful in dismantling habituation to give room for alternative decisions. For instance, the *Ruler Exercise* (Ciarrocchi, 2001) is used to assess the client's ambivalence and can be used continually throughout the therapeutic process. Start by explaining to the client that two walls will be used to assess their current state of ambivalence; one wall in the room represents 0 (not at all), while the adjacent wall represents 10 (extremely). Then ask the client to stand in the room where they are in terms of a specific issue (i.e., a door that won't close, a goal they can't commit to outside of therapy, etc.). For example, a client who wants recovery but who has relapsed would pair recovery with the wall representing 10, whereas gambling use would be paired with the wall representing 0. Ask the client to stand somewhere along the "continuum" (from 0–10) in the room. Once they find their spot, look to see where the client stands, and what direction or which wall they face. If they don't face either wall, notice the ambivalence they are experiencing. Then ask the client: What needs to happen to turn towards the 10? What needs to happen to go one number higher? Rather than focus on going from wherever they are immediately to a 10, focus the conversation on what going from a 6 to a 7 looks like for them.

Chasing Losses and Wins

Often, those struggling with a gambling disorder report knowing about chasing prior to the therapist bringing up the concept; in fact, in our experience most clients know chasing too well. Therapists should always be vigilant when discussing chasing, and ask about both chasing wins and chasing losses. Chasing wins occurs when gamblers win, but the magnitude of the win (or the total amount won) isn't "big enough" (i.e., cognitive distortion of "bigger win is coming" is all too common). During discussions about chasing, therapists should consider getting clients to reflect on what happens when they chase wins vs. chase losses. Do they place bigger bets (which in turns results in them getting closer to a negative bank)? What thoughts do they experience when they chase losses vs. wins? Do they think a win is forthcoming? What happens to their behavior when they chase? Do they place larger (or riskier) bets? How many times do they cash out when they are up? Questions that probe more deeply into what the gambling episode looks like (reduced to each decision point) will help paint a picture of the cognitive distortions, habits, and other avoidance or access patterns of the client.

To target chasing, beyond having a conversation, therapists can consider using a range of therapeutic techniques. For instance, *imaginal desensitization* can be used to combat cognitive distortions related to chasing wins or losses. Here, therapists would have the client think about and visualize themselves gambling, focusing on what happens when they notice themselves chasing wins or losses (i.e., What thoughts do you have? What feelings do you experience? What behaviors do you engage in?), and then visualize themselves engaging in different decisions (e.g., cashing out and leaving the casino; turning off phone/mobile device). Similarly, *mindfulness exercises* can be combined and/or used independently to help clients with contacting the present moment and engaging in alternative behavioral patterns rather than gambling. In mindfulness-based cognitive-behavioral therapy, *urge surfing* can also be an effective strategy to assist clients who experience the urge to chase losses/wins while using mindfulness to stay connected to the moment and abstain from gambling. Finally, *motivational interviewing* can also be useful to check in for ambivalence when it comes to acting upon different decisions instead of chasing wins/losses.

Session Considerations

Each session, therapists working with disordered gamblers must review financial restitution plans, spending, and whether the client gambled or not between sessions. If the client is working on harm reduction, therapists should check in on specifics of gambling behaviors: did the client meet their goals for spending limit or time limit? If the client is working on abstinence, therapists should check in on specifics of urges to gamble, believability of thoughts to gamble, and what worked for them on choosing not to gamble (this will also open the door to allow the client to tell the therapist of a relapse). Therapists should always keep an eye towards helping the client learn how to solve problems, and finding creative adaptive coping and/or self-soothing strategies as a replacement for gambling.

Treatment Selection

According to the literature (see Chapter 3: Models of Intervention), effica-cious treatments include cognitive-behavioral therapy (CBT; Petry, 2005), motivational interviewing (Yakovenko *et al.*, 2015), and mindfulness-based intervention strategies (Griffiths, Shonin, & Van Gordon, 2016). Therapists should consider learning about tools and techniques within each of these treatments to use with disordered gamblers. However, therapists should always consider the client's needs and the pathway to gambling before selecting a treatment strategy.

When considering the pathways model, treatment strategies can be theoretically scaffolded to consider symptoms and "subtypes" of gamblers. For instance, behaviorally conditioned gamblers (i.e., those impacted by pathway of accessibility/availability, reinforcement schedules and condi-tioning of gambling stimuli, habituation, and chasing) may respond well to CBT-related techniques such as urge surfing, decision points, challenging cognitive distortions, and imaginal desensitization. Emotionally and biolog-ical vulnerable gamblers may benefit from CBT techniques plus additional calming and soothing strategies such as mindfulness or acceptance-based techniques. Clients with co-occurring disorders (e.g., impulse control, mood disorders, antisocial and related personality disorders, etc.) must receive treatment for the co-occuring mental health disorder as well as the gambling disorder.

Mindfulness in Session

While mindfulness strategies can be a helpful self-soothing strategy, we recommend bringing mindfulness in later on in the therapeutic relationship, after understanding how the client is able to problem-solve and self-initiate self-soothing or calming strategies (or not); the client's history and potential experience of trauma, power, and control, etc. In this way, therapists ensure that they start where the client is comfortable, rather than where the therapist *wants* the client to be. For instance, if trust is an issue for the client, thera-pists shouldn't require clients to close their eyes for a 15-minute meditation;

similarly, if sitting is uncomfortable for the client, therapists should allow the client to get up and move, or lie down if possible, etc.

Therapists should consider starting mindfulness slow and easy; for some clients, this may mean starting with a body scan to assist clients who need more explicit instructions for how to calm themselves and relax. For others, this may mean starting with a guided meditation/mindfulness session with an electronic application device so that the client can continue to practice mindfulness between sessions. The best rule of thumb is to start small (under three minutes in the beginning), and rather than forcing it every session, bring it in when targeting a specific gambling symptom (i.e., cognitive distortions or decision points) or when considering relapse prevention.

For example, a mindful eating exercise can be done with any type of food or drink (e.g., cookies, fruit, chips, tea/coffee, etc.). Start by placing a single serving of the food or drink in front of the client (it helps if the therapist has their own to model and experience alongside the client) and taking a few deep breaths. Next, ask the client to think about where the food or drink came from; all the people who had to interact with the food/drink in order for it to go from one form in one geographic location to the way the food/drink is served in another geographic location. After a few more slow, deep breaths, ask the client to notice the food/drink using all their senses. What does it look like? What does it feel like? What does it smell like? What does it sound like? Before exploring taste, slow the process of consuming the food/drink into microscopic steps, allowing the client to slowly progress through before consuming a small bit of the food/drink. During consumption, ask the client to notice what the experience of eating/drinking is. Where do they feel which parts of the eating/drinking experience? Does it change across the body or over time? What about the anticipation of the next bite/drink? What is that experience like?

Relapse Prevention

Often, therapists report that they are not ready for what to do when or if their client relapses. It is important to understand that relapse is part of the recovery process and not necessarily a sign of "failure." Similar to other behaviors and symptoms related to gambling, consider relapse as a "target behaviour" if you like; this will help to consider it a part of treatment, similar to other behaviors, such as cognitive distortions (e.g., "Well, I already bet on the game, so why not place in-game bets?").

In order to help reduce the likelihood of relapsing, therapists should:

- Discuss the concept of relapse with the client, including general aspects such as what it is, why it happens to people in recovery, and how to plan/prepare for it. Plan for this discussion when the client is actively engaged in abstinence.
- Develop a list of warning signs that signal to the client they are at risk for relapsing. Warning signs can be settings or environments (i.e., work vs. sports bar), people (i.e., specific friends or family), calendar events (i.e., anniversaries, holidays, sporting events), feeling states (i.e., anxious, stressed, bored), financial situations (i.e., access to cash, loss of money or debts, etc.).
- Always honor the client's voice when discussing relapse, by providing empathetic listening, MI techniques, and other positive/affirming ways. Tell clients that therapy is a "judgment-free zone." When a client shows or displays fear or uncertainty in sharing the truth, remind them that relapse is part of the process and thank them for their honesty when they share about relapsing.
- Ask family members to attend a session (if they are not already doing family therapy) to review relapse warning signs for accuracy and accountability.
- Increase the frequency of sessions if warning signs emerge, or if some of the known triggers identified are occurring or are soon to occur (i.e., triggers based on calendar year). For instance, for sports-betting clients, the start of the play-offs can be very triggering, so increasing the dose of treatment during that time can help clients stay successful at abstaining from gambling.

Remember that if (or when) a client relapses, the therapist should start by thanking them for being honest and sharing their experience (see also the third point above). It is also important to explicitly tell the client that you (the therapist) are in this with them, and together you and the client will continue to help figure out a new way forward. For instance, in a powerful exercise for relapse, *Every Step*, the therapist goes through all decision points that led to the relapse. After identifying all steps the client took before the first bet was placed, the therapist goes through each step, asking the client to visualize every single step they took, and rehearse visualizing a new decision. The goal is to help the client visualize each decision point as a new opportunity to engage in a different behavioral pattern, in order to abstain from engaging in old patterns of behavior (i.e., habituation).

Therapists should also problem-solve with the client to figure out what doors were left open. Are there any doors the client forgot about? Are there any doors the client wasn't aware of, until after relapse? It is imperative that therapists remain neutral and non-judgmental, staying mindful and vigilant of the potential for countertransference during this process. Seeking peer supervision or consultation as needed should be considered for working effectively with gambling disorders.

Finally, but perhaps most importantly, therapists should constantly (and consistently) assess the needs of the client, and the extent to which the client needs higher levels of care. Is the client receiving an adequate dose or amount of therapy/intervention? Does the client need higher levels of care, such as inpatient treatment? Sometimes, relapse is a sign that a larger dose of therapy is needed; at other times, a different therapeutic approach is all that is needed. Figuring out the difference is a clinical competency that is unique to each client who sits in front of the therapist. It is therefore up to the therapist to seriously assess the degree to which the client's gambling symptoms/severity is worsening and becoming more threatening to the client and/or others in the client's life. Ultimately, relapse is not a reflection on the therapist. It is, however, a sign for the therapist to re-evaluate 1) the severity of symptoms, 2) the intervention strategies used and efficacy of strategies on reducing gambling severity, and 3) the adequate level of care for the client's current needs. Checking in regularly with the client to determine if they need higher levels of care is also a good way to see if a client is getting closer to hitting their short-term and long-term treatment goals.

Terminating the Therapeutic Relationship

As with all clients, therapists will more than likely reach a point where they no longer believe there is a working therapeutic alliance with their client. Terminating any therapeutic relationship should always be addressed and approached in a unique and idiosyncratic way. When considering when or if to terminate a therapeutic relationship, consider the following:

- Seek peer consultation. This is very important to ensure the therapist follows and adheres to specific credentialed/state- or country-specific ethical rules around client termination. Peer consultation can assist therapists in finding any holes or missed issues or questions involved in case conceptualization, and help therapists to assess objectively the issue of countertransference specifically related to gambling issues.
- Therapists should terminate the relationship after repeated relapse *only if* there is reason to believe the client has lied about gambling use during the therapeutic relationship. If the client relapses multiple times but continues to attend therapy and is honest about gambling use, this may not result in terminating the relationship. However, if the client relapses but lies about it in therapy for weeks or months afterwards, therefore violating the therapeutic relationship, then termination would be reasonable, especially if the client refuses a higher level of care.
- When terminating the relationship, offer referrals to other therapists with gambling expertise as appropriate.

Conclusion

This chapter has provided an overview for therapists on using evidence-informed research strategies in their clinical practice. Key factors for treating problem and at-risk gamblers include cognitive distortions, habituation to gambling games and related aspects of gambling behaviors, calming strategies, and decision points. Each of these aspects of the client's day-to-day life is impacted by the extent to which the client and therapist "close all the doors."

Treatment considerations should focus on addressing the underlying symptoms of gambling, rather than only relying on reducing the gambling behaviors. For instance, pros and cons of stopping gambling can provide therapists with a look into aspects of the client's life that are valued, yet not fully accessed or enjoyed by the client. Finding these small aspects of the client's life may open them to the possibility of the potential that they *can* engage in a different behavior at a decision point; they *can* relapse once and choose not to continue to gamble that day, therefore challenging cognitive distortions that result in persistent use; they *can* stay calm during stressful events/situations by using mindfulness/meditation strategies rather than gamble to de-stress. Change is possible, and sometimes the smallest changes lead to the biggest outcomes.

CHAPTER 5

WHERE TO START AND WHAT TO ASK

"This entire process can be anxious-making for both of us."

The purpose of this chapter is to help provide structure and guidance on where to start and what to ask when working with individuals with problematic or disordered gambling. Oftentimes, trainees anxiously will ask what they should do first, second, and third when they get their first gambling client. This chapter will give guidance on the many things to consider and assess in the early stages of the therapeutic relationship. This chapter does not distinguish between first call and intake assessment, as we could not possibly cover all the scenarios and ways people will seek care. Instead, we will discuss and highlight evidence-informed psychometric assessments and diagnostic screens/tools to incorporate into the treatment of individuals with a gambling disorder. Finally, the current chapter will provide insight into what to do at the first few appointments, and how to gather information to provide treatment that is tailored to the client's idiosyncratic needs and pathways to use.

Gambling Screens, Assessments, and Diagnostic Tools

There are many screens used to identify whether an individual may have a problem with gambling. Often these screens are done early in the intake process and could be done by someone else as part of the process to determine what level of care is needed and how to refer the client for care. The following section highlights various tools, including the Diagnostic Statistical Manual 5 (DSM-5; American Psychological Association, 2013) and the World Health Organization's (2018) ICD-10 checklist, and additional assessments that have been shown to have good levels of reliability and validity. Further, the included screens and assessments ask more targeted questions about gambling behavior, and provide severity cutoff scores, which are clinically helpful and useful in establishing a case conceptualization plan for the client.

Lie-Bet Questionnaire

The Lie-Bet screen (Johnson *et al.*, 1988) has been around for decades. It's a two-question screening for problem gambling:

- Have you ever felt the need to bet more and more money?
- Have you ever lied to people important to you about how much you gambled?

If the client responds with "yes" to one or both questions, a further evaluation would be conducted. A more recent single-item assessment was developed by Thomas, Piterman, and Jackson (2008), wherein clients are asked: "In the past 12 months, have you ever had an issue with your gambling?" If the client answers yes, then additional screening and assessments would be completed.

Brief Biosocial Gambling Screen (BBGS)

The BBGS (Gebauer, LaBrie, & Shaffer, 2010) is a three-question brief screening instrument that helps a person decide whether they need to seek a more formal evaluation or treatment of their gambling issues:

- During the past 12 months, have you become restless, irritable, or anxious when trying to stop or cut down on gambling?
- During the past 12 months, have you tried to keep your family or friends from knowing how much you gambled?

- During the past 12 months, did you have such financial trouble as a result of your gambling that you had to get help with living expenses from family friends or welfare?

If the answer is "yes" to one or more questions, a further evaluation is needed.

Both the Lie-Bet and the Brief Biosocial Gambling Screen (BBGS) are short and easy, and provide direction on whether to conduct a more thorough evaluation of someone's gambling behavior. After initial screening, subsequent screens and diagnostic checklists can and should be employed.

GBIRT

GBIRT (Gambling Brief Intervention and Referral to Treatment) was adapted from several sources, including the DSM-5, BBGS, and Dr. Elizabeth Hartney. It was developed to help professionals in various settings, including clinical practice, based on SBIRT (Screening, Brief Intervention, and Referral to Treatment; SBIRT, n.d.). SBIRT is an evidence-based practice used to screen and conduct brief intervention and referral to treatment for substance use and abuse. GBIRT was developed in part through comparison analyses that highlighted the utility of SBIRT for problem gambling. It is recommended for use in settings where services for mental health, addiction, or co-occurring disorders are delivered. In this way, GBIRT is used to implement a quick screen for problem gambling to identify any gambling-related harms that could be included in a holistic treatment.

> Gatekeeper question: "Most people gamble. In the last year about how many times did you play slot machines or video poker, or poker for money, or buy a lottery ticket or a scratch-off, or bet on a sports event, play keno or bingo, or play craps for money or play blackjack for money or go to a casino or play the stock market or do any other sort of betting or gambling?"

The question does not need to be asked verbatim. However, normalizing gambling and naming several ways that people gamble is key.

If the answer is five or more times per year, proceed to step 1. If the answer is less than five times per year, do *Brief Intervention* and complete *screen.*

Step 1

During the past year...

1   Have you tried to hide how much you have gambled from your family or friends?

2   Have you had to ask other people for money to help deal with financial problems that have been caused by gambling?

3   Have you ever felt restless, on edge, or irritable when trying to stop or cut down on gambling?

If one or more questions in step 1 are endorsed positively—"yes," proceed to step 2. If the answer to all three questions is "no," do *Brief Intervention* and complete *screen.*

Step 2

During the past year...

1   Have you tried to cut down or stop your gambling?

2   Have you increased your bet or how much you would spend, in order to feel the same kind of excitement as before?

3   Did you think about gambling even when you are not doing it (remembering past gambling experiences, or planning future gambling)?

4   Did you go to gamble when you were feeling down, stressed, angry, or bored?

5   Did you ever try to win back the money that you had recently lost?

6   Has your gambling caused problems in your relationships or with work?

If four or more questions in step 2 are endorsed positively—"yes," conduct referral to treatment. If answer to five or more questions is "no," do *Brief Intervention* and complete *screen*.

Simply Asking Open-Ended Questions (Fun Assessment)

This is not a new concept and does not require an evidence-based assessment to validate. In clinical practice, it may be a "new" way to screen and look for clues with clients regarding their gambling behaviors. This is often most helpful for clients who do not actively seek help for a gambling problem, but still warrant a thorough evaluation that includes gambling behavior. When asking individuals if they gamble or buy lottery tickets, or other more direct questions related to gambling, individuals may not answer truthfully as they hear the question in the context of why they are seeking immediate help. When therapists ask open-ended questions as part of getting to know the client, the client may share clues and hints about gambling activities and behaviors that may become problematic when their reason for seeking help is resolved. Think of this as a "Fun Assessment"; it will not only give therapists an understanding of the client's strengths and protective behaviors, but also highlight areas that can become or are already risk factors.

- What do you do for fun, enjoyment, hobbies now?
- How do you like to celebrate?
- How do you calm down, unwind, relax?
- What did you do for fun, enjoyment, hobbies in the past?
- Who do you go out/socialize with? Where do you go?
- What loss have you experienced in the past six months?
- What hard decisions have you had to make about money?
- What games do you like to play (board games/cards/video)?
- What makes you laugh?
- What makes you cry?
- What are your favorite foods?
- What do you do for entertainment?

- When do you have the most energy?
- What do you do when you're bored?
- How many hours is the TV on in your home each day?

For any questions, therapists are looking for answers indicating that gambling is a common or frequent activity or the individual may become at risk for a gambling problem without education and brief intervention.

Diagnostic Statistical Manual-5 (DSM-5)

The DSM-IV included problem gambling in the Impulse Control Disorder section where it was called Pathological Gambling. With the release of the DSM-5 (American Psychiatric Association, 2013), problem gambling was reclassified as a Substance Use Disorder, in the Behavioral Addictions subsection, and renamed Gambling Disorder. Gambling Addiction and Compulsive Gambling are terms also used to describe a gambling disorder. Gambling Disorder criteria in the DSM-5 (Criteria 312.31 (F63.0)) requires at least four of nine criteria to be met in the past year for the diagnosis:[1]

1   Needs to gamble with increasing amounts of money in order to achieve the desired excitement.

2   Is restless or irritable when attempting to cut down or stop gambling.

3   Has made repeated unsuccessful efforts to control, cut back, or stop gambling.

4   Is often preoccupied with gambling (e.g., having persistent thoughts of reliving past gambling experiences, handicapping or planning the next venture, thinking of ways to get money with which to gamble).

5   Often gambles when feeling distressed (e.g., helpless, guilty, anxious, depressed).

6   After losing money gambling, often returns another day to get even ("chasing" one's losses).

7   Lies to conceal the extent of involvement with gambling.

8   Has jeopardized or lost a significant relationship, job, or educational or career opportunity because of gambling.

9   Relies on others to provide money to relieve desperate financial situations caused by gambling.

An additional change when moving to DSM-5 was the removal of one criterion involving committing illegal acts. "Has committed illegal acts such as forgery, fraud, theft, or embezzlement to finance gambling" was removed, not because individuals weren't committing crimes to support their gambling, but because engaging in criminal acts (or not) wouldn't change the extent to which the person would be diagnosed.

International Statistical Classification of Diseases and Related Health Problems (ICD-11)

The World Health Organization (WHO) established the International Statistical Classification of Diseases and Related Health Problems (11th edition; ICD-11; World Health Organization, 2019); it defines gambling disorder as characterized by:[2]

1   Preoccupation with gambling (or always thinking about gambling)

2   Lying about gambling

3   Spending work or family time gambling

---

2   Reproduced with permission from *International Statistical Classification of Diseases and Related Health Problems, 11th ed*, World Health Organization, 2019.

4   Feeling bad after gambling, but not quitting

5   Gambling with money needed for other things (i.e., rent, bills, gas, food, etc.).

Pathological Gambling (312.31) was replaced with Gambling Disorder (F63.0) with DSM-5. ICD-11 kept the term Pathological Gambling but also references the term Gambling Disorder.

South Oaks Gambling Screen (SOGS)

The SOGS (Lesieur & Blume, 1987) is a 26-item questionnaire (20 of which are scored) originally based on the DSM-III criteria for pathological gambling. The screen can be self-administered or administered by non-professional or professional interviewers. It is a psychometric instrument widely used internationally to assess the presence of pathological gambling. Scores range from 0 to 20, where scores of 5 or higher are characterized as indicators of pathological gambling. This assessment has good internal and convergent validity (Stinchfield, 2002; Stinchfield & Winters, 2001) for both clinical and general populations (Gambino & Lesieur, 2006; Stinchfield, 2002). Because of its continued reliability and validity, the SOGS is still used today to develop cutoff scores and determine the severity of a probable gambling disorder.

Problem Gambling Severity Index (PGSI)

The PGSI (Ferris & Wynne, 2001) was developed as an alternative to the SOGS (Holtgraves, 2009). This nine-item questionnaire is used to measure the severity of gambling problems. Cutoff scores determine four subgroups of gamblers: non-problem (0), low risk (1–2), moderate risk (3–7), and problem gambler (8+). The PGSI has been shown to have good test–retest and internal reliability (Ferris & Wynne, 2001), and has been shown to be positively correlated with frequency of gambling (Holtgraves, 2009).

Gambling Pathways Questionnaire (GPQ)

The GPQ (Nower & Blaszczynski, 2017) was developed from the pathways model (see Chapter 2: Understanding Gambling Disorder) to establish etiological subtypes of problem gamblers. The authors studied 1176 treatment-seeking problem gamblers in Canada, the United States, and Australia. Gamblers completed the 48-item questionnaire, categorized across six factors (i.e., anti-social, impulsive risk-taking; stress-coping; childhood maltreatment; mood pre-problem gambling; mood post-problem gambling; and meaning motivation), by using a six point Likert-scale (ranging from 1 = strongly disagree to 6 = strongly agree). While research using the questionnaire is still in early stages, results from the 2017 study found high internal consistency and moderate construct validity for etiological factors as categorized within the pathways model (e.g., Blaszczynski & Nower, 2002). Gambler's scores are totalled across each pathway, and total scores are compared relatively across the three pathways.

Gambling Functional Assessment II (GFA-II)

The GFA-II (Dixon *et al.*, 2018) is a ten-item questionnaire that was developed to identify environmental consequences that maintain gambling, including escape or avoidance from painful or aversive people, places, or things; social attention; access to tangible rewards including money, complimentary amenities or "comps" (i.e., free hotel rooms or restaurant experiences), and vouchers; and enhanced sensory experiences including feeling a rush or "buzz" when gambling. Gamblers respond to items using a seven-point Likert scale (0 = never to 6 = always), and scores are totaled across categories (i.e., sensory, escape, attention, and tangible). Research to date has found increased total scores on the GFA-II to be correlated with increased gambling severity (as measured by the SOGS, r=.55).

The Chicken or the Egg: Which Came First?

As part of a thorough evaluation, it is important to determine where gambling occurs on the timeline of the client. It is essential to screen for mental health, injuries, and chemical use that may have developed prior to or after the problematic gambling.

Depression and Anxiety

The *Patient Health Questionnaire-9* (PHQ-9; Kroenke, Spitzer, & Williams, 2001) is the nine-item depression module of the longer Patient Health Questionnaire. It is a self-administered tool for assessing depression during the past two weeks using a Likert scale from not at all (0) to nearly every day (3). There are five Depression Severity Types based on the score and they all warrant further evaluation for clinical diagnosis. The total score is interpreted as follows: minimal depression (1–4), mild depression (5–9), moderate depression (10–14), moderately severe depression (15–19) and severe depression (20–27). More importantly, therapists must review Question 9 of the PHQ-9 (i.e., "Thoughts that you would be better off dead or of hurting yourself") with their client to determine suicide risk. Answering anything other than "Not at all" would result in the therapist conducting an immediate suicide risk assessment (see below for additional information).

The *Generalized Anxiety Disorder* scale (GAD-7; Spitzer *et al.*, 2006) is a seven-item screening tool and symptom severity measure for the four most common anxiety disorders (e.g., Generalized Anxiety, Panic, Social Phobia, and Post Traumatic Stress). Similar to the PHQ-9, it assesses symptoms in the past two weeks, using a Likert scale from not at all (0) to nearly every day (3). Scores of 10 and higher warrant a further clinical assessment for diagnosis.

Using these two mental health screens (PHQ-9 and GAD-7) is important as it allows the therapist to begin assessing for any undiagnosed, untreated, or under-treated mental health disorder(s) where gambling is acting as self-medicating and secondary. Therapists can also use other evidence-based screens.

Traumatic Brain Injuries (TBI)

Traumatic brain injuries, or TBIs, include any injury to the brain including concussion, physical assault, or other brain injury that needs to be evaluated as part of a gambling evaluation. Previous research has identified that behavioral effects such as disinhibition, impulsiveness and obsessive behavior, and cognitive effects including memory loss and impaired reasoning can make brain injury survivors more vulnerable to the addictive nature of gambling (Headway: The Brain Injury Association, 2020).

Trauma such as childhood, sexual, military/combat, and domestic/intimate partner violence needs to be evaluated as part of the comprehensive explanation of a gambling disorder. Early research showed that a link exists between trauma/stress and gambling disorders (McKinlay *et al.*, 1981), and this is still true today (e.g., Hodgins *et al.*, 2010; Imperatori *et al.*, 2017; Kausch, Rugal, & Rowland, 2006). The topic of trauma can be very sensitive for so many and it may not be appropriate to ask too early in the therapeutic relationship, but make sure to revisit when the alliance is stronger and the environment feels safe to the client. The key is to thoroughly assess trauma for anyone seeking help for a gambling problem.

Drugs, Alcohol, Nicotine/Tobacco, and Cannabis

Depending on the clinical setting, therapists may already have all of the chemical use information. In outpatient and private practice settings, it is important to fully assess all addictive behaviors and their potential association with problem gambling. First, therapists will want to assess the severity of drug and alcohol use in the event the client needs a higher level of care for medical reasons. Many family members don't understand the importance of medical care for alcohol addiction since withdrawal can be fatal if not medically managed properly. Asking about drug and alcohol use will also help to determine the cross-interaction, if any, with gambling. For example, every time the client gambles, they then compulsively drink alcohol. Or the client only gambles when using cannabis, and so on. Develop an artful way to inquire about drinking, using, and smoking to keep the client from feeling judgment and shame. Get curious about how, when, with whom, how often, in what quantities, and whether there is a pattern or theme connecting to their gambling behavior. Practice using words like "cannabis" instead of marijuana, "nicotine" instead of cigarettes and smoking, and "beer/liquor/wine/mixed drinks" instead of alcohol. Depending on the client, therapists may find it helpful to share research about the brain and co-occurring disorders while asking about drug and alcohol use (see also Chapter 2: Understanding Gambling Disorder). For instance, research has shown that smoking tobacco is not only common among problem gamblers, but is also correlated with higher urges to gamble (Grant & Potenza, 2005). Similarly, research has found that gamblers undergoing treatment who continue to use nicotine while abstinent from gambling have higher relapse rates at six months (Grant *et al.*, 2005).

Suicide Risk Assessment

Individuals with a gambling disorder are at a higher risk for suicidal ideation and death by suicide than the national average (Giovanni *et al.*, 2017). Researchers have found a direct relationship between gambling and suicidality; the combination of impulsivity, certain psychiatric disorders, and social factors explains the frequent occurrence of suicidal behavior (Giovanni *et al.*, 2017). Ask and talk about suicidality with clients from the first meeting and regularly throughout therapy. Therapists can choose to prompt the conversation from Question 9 of the PHQ-9 or discuss suicidality at the beginning of the full evaluation; it doesn't matter as long as therapists ask always and act if necessary. Remember to ask directly about suicidal thoughts and use words like "kill yourself." Always start with the past 12 months, with questions about "thoughts," "plan," and then "attempts." See the sample Gambling Biopsycho-social-Spiritual Evaluation later in this chapter for specific questions. Develop standard practices of having every client program the suicide helpline into their cell/smartphone as a contact. This replaces handing someone a handout/pamphlet with the helpline number on it. There is no guarantee they will have the pamphlet readily available if/when they need the 800-number.

Gambling Problem or Gambling Solution

When developing case conceptualization during the full evaluation, consider which profile fits the client: "Gambling Problem" or "Gambling Solution." A Gambling Problem profile includes other psychiatric features or disorders, other addictive behaviors or addictions, history of impulsivity, and genetic vulnerabilities. A Gambling Solution profile includes avoidance coping skills, past trauma, poor problem-solving skills, and overall sense of dependency and lack of control over the environment. Understanding these two profiles can aid in development of treatment goals and treatment planning in terms of where to start and what is the end goal. For example, the Gambling Solution client requires understanding of the "other problems or issues" that have been unresolved for so long that gambling originally was the way to avoid those problems. This can be an unhappy relationship/marriage, empty nest, "fork in the road," or unresolved trauma where gambling became the dissociation mechanism. Once the therapist and client deal with and/or resolve the "other problem," gambling no longer serves the same purpose. A Gambling Problem client is considered someone with "addictive" behaviors, lifestyle, and genetic predisposition. It doesn't matter what day of the week, what month of the year, or what the temperature is outside—actively gambling is always compulsive and difficult to cut down or stop without intervention.

Closing the Doors

"Closing the doors" to access, availability, and opportunity to gamble is an easy concept for clients to grasp and it becomes a shared vocabulary between the therapist and the client. As part of being curious during evaluations, therapists can assist with identifying all the "doors" that need to be closed to help the client reduce harm and/or abstain from problematic gambling. This shared vocabulary also helps the client to gain insight into healthier ways to solve problems in the future. Many of the doors are centered around access to gambling and access to money. More specifically, bank accounts, credit cards, cash, online gambling sites, bookies, local gambling venues, and smartphones can be doors to continued problematic gambling and negative consequences. Establish a non-threatening dialogue with clients to support them and to help them close all the doors so they can focus on reaching their goals and restoring trust with family and friends. Focusing on all the doors from a tactical level first gives structure to the first few sessions together. It is a roadmap with measurable checkpoints.

It's a Control Thing

Having worked with substance-use disorders prior to gambling disorders, it became obvious to us that problematic and disordered gambling has an extreme element of control. Consider talking about control with clients so that when it shows up in the session, you can call it and help the client gain insight and awareness. Metaphors are helpful in educating clients about control and gambling. For example, talk about control as odorless, colorless, invisible gas/smoke—if you could give it color, you would see how much of it was in the room, taking up space and making it so difficult to focus on anything else. Control often appears when discussing closing "doors" related to finances or access to gambling. It can feel like a ping-pong match or, worse yet, trying to "nail jello to the wall" if you don't introduce a shared vocabulary. Respect that control is a protective mechanism and being able to talk about control is often key in the therapeutic alliance.

Creating a Safe Place

This may seem like an obvious topic, but it is one that can't be discussed enough. So often, we, as therapists, forget what it is like to show up for therapy for the first time: anxious, self-loathing, feeling shame, and very down and depressed. Is there anything to do to make the session environment feel safer? For example, certain pictures or posters, where you sit relative to where the client sits (distance), and whether you establish good eye contact with body posture that is relaxed yet self-assured. What do you typically say to your clients at the beginning of the first meeting or at the end of the first session? Is it procedural or is it more accepting and instilling hope for the future? All of these things need to match your personality and temperament, and be consistent with future sessions as you are role-modeling how words and actions need to match accountability and responsibility. Consider using certain phrases, at the appropriate times, to ease the anxiety and negative self-talk of your clients: "This is a judgment-free zone and your safe space to share difficult things and know that you will get better over time." Share about your gambling addiction training and why you like to work with this disorder. Talk about how gambling is everywhere and so socially acceptable, and about how you are here to help those that ask for help. All of these small actions and purposefully chosen words will add up and help your client become more relaxed and hopefully more honest over time.

The First Few Sessions

This section is designed to assist therapists in developing their own process when working with problematic and disordered gambling. Use the tools and processes discussed in this chapter to create your own thorough and comprehensive approach to treating this disorder. Information shared in this section was adapted from *Overcoming Pathological Gambling: Therapist Guide* by R. Ladouceur and S. Lachance (2007).

Where to Start and What to Ask

You have introduced yourself to your client, welcomed them into your office, and you both sit down. What next? Inquire about their reason for seeking therapy at this time. What led them to want to get help now? Have they ever had gambling therapy before and, if so, where and how long ago? Ask them how they came to see you. Inquiring about "why you" is often helpful in understanding the way that they asked for help. It is helpful to see how they go about solving their problems—for example, they may have found an advertisement in *Psychology Today*, called an 800 helpline number or their insurance, or even got your name from a family member. Consider giving an overview of how the session will go. You might say something like "I'm going to ask a lot of questions this session and we will talk about my initial impressions and recommendations at the end of this session." Review any paperwork that was completed prior to the appointment, such as screens, PHQ-9 and GAD-7, and other paperwork deemed necessary by your place of work. When you're reviewing this paperwork, take every opportunity to provide some education that helps the client begin to understand any connections with their gambling behavior.

If you're in a small group practice or private practice setting, this is the time to conduct your gambling biopsychosocial-spiritual evaluation. If you are in another setting, you may already have some of the following sections of information located on other forms as required by your employer.

Presence of Suicidal Ideation

Complete this section early in the session in case the client is suicidal and you need to take action to get them into a higher level of care. Ask questions, including: In the past 12 months have you ever seriously thought about attempting suicide? If yes, have you thought about a way to do it? Was the thought mainly linked to your gambling problems? Did you attempt suicide in the last 12 months? Have you ever attempted suicide? If yes, what year and explain the context. And last, are you presently considering suicide or thoughts of harming yourself or others? At this time, encourage the client to program the local suicide or crisis helpline number into their phone. Remember: thoughts of suicide can occur at any time, and having the crisis helpline number already programmed into the phone is far more effective than handing the person a pamphlet with the phone number written on it.

Motivation and Consequences of Gambling

Inquire what aspects of their gambling behavior have led them to consult with you. Look for how motivated they are to undertake measures to resolve their gambling. Determine if there's a specific reason or event that motivated them to seek help: relationships, family/parents, partner/ spouse, friends, work, finances, legal, or other reasons. Assess the motivation level with the severity of the consequences. Determine if their gambling problem has caused them to become "out of sync developmentally and chronologically," especially with "failure to launch" individuals. Are they experiencing physical health issues as a result of their gambling (sleep or weight issues, headaches)? Inquire if they have any problems at work or serious employment issues related to their gambling behavior.

Games/Gambling

Ask about each and every type of gambling activity to understand which ones they are currently having difficulty controlling and which ones may have been a precursor form of gambling. Differentiate between lotteries and scratch-offs, casino slots and casino table games, online gambling and sports betting, and video games and games on smartphones or via Facebook and social casino games.

Development of Gambling Habits

Ask about an early "big win" experience and how much they won, the amount of the bet, and how long ago was this. Inquire about the people who introduced them to gambling: parents, grandparents, aunts/uncles, siblings, friends, neighbors, work colleagues, and others, and in their opinion, how old they were when they believed gambling became a problem and what triggered the gambling problem.

Current Gambling Problem

Determine the main reasons or issues that motivate them to gamble at this point. Are they looking to distract from, change, or escape daily problems and stresses? Are they trying to make money or resolve a financial problem due to gambling? Do they gamble for the rush and excitement? Boredom? Are there any other reasons that they might identify as main reasons to gamble currently. Obtain an average of how much time they spend each week gambling, and how much money they spend gambling in a given week.

DSM-5 Diagnostic Criteria and Other Assessments

Share with your client that you're going to be asking a series of questions and you would like them to answer with a "yes" or "no" to each question. Review each of the nine criteria for gambling disorder in the DSM-5. At the end, add up the score and share with the client. Explain that a score of four or more indicates they meet the criteria for gambling disorder. You may want to complete the PGSI to determine the level of severity and the pathways model to determine subtype.

Finances

Ask about their financial situation and introduce the idea of getting more involved in their current financial situation in later sessions. Determine if they have a history of bankruptcy—when, for how much, and whether it was related to their gambling. Get an initial overview of all their debt, whom they owe, and how much. Also assess their relationship with money and baseline financial literacy.

Current Living Conditions

Inquire about their current lifestyle including living conditions, diet, relationships, hobbies, and work. Ask if they are currently using any community services for food, clothing, or utility assistance. Don't make assumptions about a client…*always ask* about community assistance. Determine if any family issues related to history of addiction, mental health, child custody visitation/arrangements, or other family dynamics currently impact their living situation.

Other Compulsive or Addictive Behaviors

You want to ask about all other behaviors that may have been, in the past or currently, problematic. You are looking for co-occurring addictions, cross-addictions, and interactive addictions. Cross-addictions will show as replacing one addiction with another addiction over time. Dual or multiple addictions will show as two or more addictions at the same point in time. An interactive addiction is typically identified with a process addiction (gambling, sex) and a chemical addiction (drugs, alcohol), where the process addiction goes undetected for a longer period of time while the chemical addiction receives targeted treatment. If multiple addictive behaviors are not properly screened and simultaneously treated, the chances of long-term recovery are reduced.

Develop a checklist for the following and determine current and/or past use or engagement. For each, determine when the problem started, for how long it was a problem, and whether the client received treatment or help.

- ✓ **Nicotine:** cigarettes, smokeless/chew, and vaping
- ✓ **Drugs**: cannabis, cocaine, opioids, methamphetamines, etc.
- ✓ **Alcohol**: beer, liquor, wine
- ✓ **Medication**: prescribed, illegal, multiple doctor scripts
- ✓ **Internet/screen time**: porn, online behaviors, etc.

✓ **Sexual activity**: multiple partners, out-of-bounds relationships, hiring prostitutes, anonymous partners, excessive masturbation, porn shops
✓ **Compulsive buying/spending**: online or brick-and-mortar shopping
✓ **Video games**: action, strategy, card/puzzle; online vs. console vs. phone/app use
✓ **eSports**: watching and/or practicing for eSports teams, competition, and scholarships
✓ **Other**: any other activities that may be excessive or problematic.

Next, you will want to understand how alcohol, drugs, or other behaviors interact with gambling. Look for a relationship before, during, and after gambling with alcohol, drugs, or behaviors and what percentage of the time it happens.

Prior Mental Health and Health Problems

If you don't have access to medical records, inquire about whether the client has consulted with a doctor, psychiatrist, or other counseling professionals for psychiatric problems. What type of specialist, when, for what reason, and what was the outcome (medication, therapy)? Obtain a thorough list of current medications, duration, and reason they were prescribed. Look for depression and anxiety medications as well as stimulants signaling prior mental health issues that need to be included in your treatment of the gambling problem. You are also looking for any medications that may have a side effect of compulsive gambling (dopamine agonist, partial agonist properties). At the time of this publication, restless leg syndrome medications (Mirapex), atypical antipsychotic medications (Abilify), and Requip® for Parkinson's disease all have warnings issued by the FDA.

Learn about current eating habits, diet, and exercise as these may become useful treatment goals when managing boredom. Also determine if there are any sleep issues or habits impacting a healthier lifestyle.

Personal Strengths and Resources

Most clinical evaluations are seeking answers to problems and problematic behaviors. Remember to also inquire about your client's strengths, supports, hobbies, and activities that are not related to gambling. In the case of hobbies, activities, and community supports, clients may have engaged in these behaviors prior to developing a gambling problem but no longer do so. Simply discussing now may help them to have hope for a better tomorrow. Make sure to include any religious or spiritual preferences as part of your treatment goals.

Steps Taken Prior to Seeking Treatment

Many clients have already taken several steps to stop their problematic gambling behavior. Have they attended 12-Step (GA) before, seen another certified gambling therapist or other addiction therapist, self-excluded, obtained financial services, or sought legal counsel?

Summary of Initial Recommendations

Before you end the session, make sure you instil hope and confidence in the client that they have come to the right person for help. You want your client to return for the next session more than you want them to do anything else after this first meeting. This disorder has a high dropout rate and you want to give them reasons to return for the next appointment. Be careful not to over-recommend things to do as the client will quickly become overwhelmed and consider not coming back. You may not have completed the Gambling Evaluation in one session. Discuss where you will pick up in the next session and reassure the client that you will be getting to know them over several sessions. Also openly talk about continued gambling and let your client know that you want them to be honest with you at all times, as it is the only way you can help them to help themselves. Remember the non-judgmental environment and reinforce that you understand this disorder and you aren't expecting them to change overnight.

When the client is very motivated, you can give them suggestions to begin the process of self-excluding, attending a GA meeting, having family/partner/spouse attend the next session, and/or beginning to collect their bills and other debts to review with you in the next few sessions. When the client is less motivated, your focus is to reduce power and control dynamics, and get them to schedule another appointment with you.

Schedule the next appointment, review any homework or things to look into, and then share that you will always be here, just a phone call away, and you are here to help. Make sure you schedule just far enough ahead on your calendar to give them time to process but not so far as to give them time to avoid returning for help. Reinforce the non-judgmental environment and your desire to help in addition to your knowledge and expertise. Give them time to ask any additional questions and treat them with the utmost respect and kindness. You are role-modeling with every word and interaction that they are worth it. This is a very high dropout group of individuals and you can't help them if they don't come back.

Clinical Impressions

Review the answers to all the questions and utilize the "person-in-environment" perspective. Consider a preliminary treatment plan that captures their strengths, gives opportunities for them to co-create the desired outcomes, and closes as many doors as possible to disordered gambling.

This chapter provides direction on where to start and what to ask, specifically related to gambling activities and behaviors. Remember to always ask and assess for suicide with this population. Conduct a thorough review of their gambling behaviors, both past and present, and determine which doors need to be closed as soon as possible in order to begin relief and recovery. Complete more than one assessment to develop a clear understanding of not only the types of gambling but also the severity and pathway of the gambling. Begin the ongoing assessment of other mental health and addictive disorders that may also need treatment and review all medications for possible side effects of excessive gambling. Create the safe space for clients to be honest and remove any judgments, shame, or stigma from the environment. Develop your initial clinical impression, share the roadmap with your client, and seek peer consultation when necessary.

The Gambling Biopsychosocial-Spiritual Evaluation is available to download from www.jkp.com/catalogue/book/9781787755529.

GAMBLING BIOPSYCHOSOCIAL-SPIRITUAL EVALUATION

Modified from Treatment Works Series, by Ladouceur and Lachance, 2007
with permission of Oxford Publishing Limited through PLSclear.

Date: . . . .

Client: . . . .   Client #: . . . .

Therapist: . . . .

Reason for seeking help: . . . .

. . . .

. . . .

PRESENCE OF SUICIDAL IDEATION

1. **In the past 12 months, have you ever SERIOUSLY thought about attempting suicide?**

    Yes ○   No ○

    a. If YES, have you thought about a way to do it?

        Yes ○   No ○

    b. Was this thought mainly linked to your gambling problems?

        Yes ○   No ○

    c. Have you attempted suicide in the last 12 months?

        Yes ○   No ○

*

2. **Have you ever attempted suicide?**

   Yes ○   No ○

   a. If YES, then what year? . . . .

   b. Explain the context: . . . .

3. **Are you presently considering suicide?**

   Yes ○   No ○

   Document thoughts to harm self or others, plan, develop safety plan,
   provide Crisis helpline:

   . . . .

   . . . .

   . . . .

   . . . .

   Is there a need for a referral for emergent care services to
   another provider?   Yes ○   No ○

   Reason:. . . . .

   . . . .

   . . . .

   . . . .

MOTIVATION OF CONSULTATION/EVALUATION

1.   **What specific event led you to consult with me?**

. . . .

. . . .

2.   **Any other reasons?**

Yes ○   No ○

Reason	Comments
Threat of separation or pressure from spouse/partner because of gambling	
Pressure from parents because of gambling	
Loss of relationships because of gambling	
Threats or pressure from employer	
Loss of employment due to gambling	
Loss of control over gambling activities	
Loss of significant possessions	
Financial problems	
Legal problems	
Other	

*

GAMES THAT LEAD TO A PARTIAL OR COMPLETE LOSS OF CONTROL

	Ever played? (Check if yes)	Do you find difficulty in controlling yourself at this game? (Check if yes)	If yes, how long have you had this difficulty? (Number of months or years)
A. Lotteries	○	○	
B. Casino	○	○	
Blackjack	○	○	
Poker	○	○	
Roulette	○	○	
Baccarat	○	○	
Keno	○	○	
Slot machines	○	○	
Sport betting (brick and mortar)	○	○	
C. Bingo	○	○	
D. Cards	○	○	
E. Horse, dog, or other types of animal racing	○	○	
F. Stock market or commodities	○	○	

G. Video lottery terminals	○	○
H. Bowling, pool, golf, or other skill games	○	○
I. Dice (craps, etc.)	○	○
J. Online sports betting	○	○
K. Internet wagering: slot, blackjack, other	○	○
L. Gambling apps	○	○
M. Video games	○	○
N. Facebook/ social casinos	○	○
O. Other	○	○

Comments:

. . . .

. . . .

. . . .

. . . .

*

INFORMATION ON THE DEVELOPMENT OF GAMBLING HABITS

1. You have told me that you have had trouble controlling your gambling in the past. When you first played these games, do you remember having a significant win, i.e. having "won big"? (Large wins within the first few experiences with the game(s) in question qualify as a "yes" in this instance.)

Yes ○   No ○

a.   If yes, how much did you win? . . . .

b.   What was the amount of the bet? . . . .

c.   How long ago was this? (specify in months or years) . . . .

d.   What did you do with the "big win"?

. . . .

. . . .

e.   What type of game were you playing? . . . .

2. **Which of the following people introduced you to gambling?
(Specify the relationship)**

○ Father   ○ Grandmother

○ Mother   ○ Spouse

○ Brother   ○ Neighbor

○ Sister   ○ Friend

○ Aunt   ○ Work Colleague

○ Uncle   ○ Myself

○ Grandfather   ○ Other (specify): . . . .

3. **How old were you when gambling became a problem for you?**

. . . .

4. **In your opinion, what triggered your gambling problem?**

. . . .

. . . .

*

INFORMATION ON CURRENT GAMBLING PROBLEM

1. **What are the main reasons or issues that motivate you to gamble at this point? (Check all that apply)**

    To distract from or escape daily problems ○

    To avoid stresses ○

    To make money ○

    To resolve a financial problem ○

    For the rush/excitement ○

    Boredom ○

    Other reason(s):

    . . . .

    . . . .

2. **On average, how much time do you spend gambling each week?**

    . . . . total hours

3. **On average, how much money do you spend gambling in one week?**

    $ . . . .

DSM-5 DIAGNOSTIC CRITERIA

You must read each item as described below. If, after reading the question below as stated, the individual does not understand, then you may reformulate the question to improve understanding. For each DSM-5 criterion, you must be able to clearly state YES or NO whether the individual meets each criterion. If doubt remains, probing might be necessary.

1. **Do you need to gamble with increasing amounts of money in order to achieve the desired excitement?**

    Yes ○   No ○

    If yes, do you have tendency to:
    a.   increase your bet

         Yes ○   No ○

    b.   always bet the maximum amount

         Yes ○   No ○

2. **Have you felt restless or irritable when attempting to cut down or stop gambling?**

    Yes ○   No ○

3. **Have you already made repeated unsuccessful efforts to control, cut back, or stop gambling?**

    Yes ○   No ○

*

If yes, please share more about what you've tried or how long you have stopped.

. . . .

. . . .

4. Do you find that you are preoccupied with gambling (e.g., having persistent thoughts of reliving past gambling experiences, handicapping or planning the next venture, thinking of ways to get money with which to gamble)?

    Yes ○   No ○

5. Do you gamble when feeling distressed (e.g., helpless, guilty, anxious, depressed)?

    Yes ○   No ○

6. After losing money gambling, do you often return another day to get even ("chase one's losses")?

    Yes ○   No ○

7. Has it happened that you have lied to conceal the extent of your involvement in gambling?

    Yes ○   No ○

8. Have you jeopardized or lost a significant relationship, job, educational or career opportunity because of gambling?

    Yes ○   No ○

If yes, did they involve...

Family relations ○   Work ○

Spousal/partner
relations ○   Friendships ○

                          Studies ○

Work relationships ○

Explain:

. . . .

. . . .

9. **Do you rely on others to provide you with money to relieve desperate financial situations caused by gambling?**

Yes ○   No ○

Number of diagnostic criteria present (9): . . . .

Please share with your client how they scored and that 4 or more meets the criteria for a Gambling Disorder.

*

CONSEQUENCES OF GAMBLING PROBLEM

At present, to what extent does your gambling behavior affect your:

Aspect of living	Comments:
1. Social Life E.g.: reduction of friends, isolation, abandoning social activities	
2. Relationships E.g.: arguments, decrease in time spent together, irritability	
3. Family life E.g.: absences, decrease in time spent with children, irritability	
4. Work/school E.g.: Lateness, lack of communication, decrease in efficiency	
5. Mood E.g.: anxiety, worries, depression	
6. Sleep E.g.: difficulty falling asleep, staying asleep, waking up too early	
7. Physical E.g.: headaches, weight gain	
8. Financial situation	
9. Spiritual	
10. Developmentally out of sync with chronological age	

1. **Have you declared bankruptcy?**

   Yes ○   No ○

   a. If yes, when?

   . . . .

   . . . .

   b. What was the amount of debt?

   . . . .

   . . . .

   c. What amount was directly related to gambling?

   . . . .

   . . . .

2. **At present, to whom do you owe money?**

   . . . .

   . . . .

   Amount owed? $ . . . .

*

CURRENT LIVING CONDITIONS

1. Describe your current lifestyle (living conditions, diet, close relationships, work, hobbies).

   . . . .

   . . . .

   . . . .

   . . . .

2. Do you use community services for food, clothing, or other essential needs for yourself or family? If yes, please explain.

   . . . .

   . . . .

   . . . .

   . . . .

3. Describe any family issues related to history of any addiction, mental health issues, child custody/visitation, childcare arrangements, or other family dynamics.

   . . . .

   . . . .

   . . . .

   . . . .

OTHER DEPENDENCIES (CURRENT AND PAST)

1. Do you currently have or have you in the past had problems with the following behaviors:

	In the past?	Current?
Cigarettes	Yes ○ No ○	Yes ○ No ○
	. . . .	
	. . . .	
Nicotine	Yes ○ No ○	Yes ○ No ○
	. . . .	
	. . . .	
Cannabis	Yes ○ No ○	Yes ○ No ○
	. . . .	
	. . . .	
Drug use	Yes ○ No ○	Yes ○ No ○
	. . . .	
	. . . .	
Alcohol	Yes ○ No ○	Yes ○ No ○
	. . . .	
	. . . .	

*

	In the past?	Current?
Medication	Yes ○ No ○	Yes ○ No ○
	. . . .	
	. . . .	
Internet	Yes ○ No ○	Yes ○ No ○
	. . . .	
	. . . .	
Compulsive sexual behaviors (porn, masturbating, etc.)	Yes ○ No ○	Yes ○ No ○
	. . . .	
	. . . .	
Compulsive buying	Yes ○ No ○	Yes ○ No ○
	. . . .	
	. . . .	
Video gaming, internet games	Yes ○ No ○	Yes ○ No ○
	. . . .	
	. . . .	
Other behaviors Specify:	Yes ○ No ○	Yes ○ No ○
	. . . .	
	. . . .	

Describe, in detail, the specific dependencies. Include when started, types of drugs, medication, and other specific behaviors, any clean/sober time and for how long.

. . . .

. . . .

. . . .

. . . .

In relation to alcohol consumption...

1. **Do you drink before gambling?**

   Yes ○   No ○

   If yes, what proportion of the time does this happen?   . . . . %

2. **Do you drink while you gamble?**

   Yes ○   No ○

   If yes, what proportion of the time does this happen?   . . . . %

3. **Do you drink after you gamble?**

   Yes ○   No ○

   If yes, what proportion of the time does this happen?   . . . . %

*

In relation to drug consumption…

1. **Do you use drugs before gambling?**

   Yes ○   No ○

   If yes, what proportion of the time does this happen?   . . . . %

2. **Do you use drugs while you gamble?**

   Yes ○   No ○

   If yes, what proportion of the time does this happen?   . . . . %

3. **Do you use drugs after you gamble?**

   Yes ○   No ○

   If yes, what proportion of the time does this happen?   . . . . %

PRESENCE OF PRIOR MENTAL HEALTH AND HEALTH PROBLEMS

1. **Have you ever consulted a doctor, psychologist, or psychiatrist for other psychiatric difficulties?**

   Yes ○   No ○

   If yes...

What type of specialist?	When?	For what reason?

   . . . .

What type of specialist?	When?	For what reason?

   . . . .

What type of specialist?	When?	For what reason?

   . . . .

2. **Are you currently taking prescribed medication?**

   Yes ○   No ○

   List medications, duration, and reason prescribed.

   . . . .

   . . . .

   . . . .

   . . . .

*

3. Describe your diet and exercise habits.

. . . .

. . . .

. . . .

. . . .

4. Describe your sleep patterns or habits.

. . . .

. . . .

. . . .

. . . .

PERSONAL STRENGTHS AND RESOURCES AVAILABLE

Review the answers to all questions and synthesize below.

1. Benefits from support from close ones, contacts, employers:

. . . .

. . . .

. . . .

. . . .

2. Shows interest in other activities not related to gambling:

. . . .

. . . .

. . . .

. . . .

3. Military—branch of service, length of service, and type of discharge:

. . . .

. . . .

. . . .

. . . .

*

4. **Attendance in 12-Step (which meetings, when, sponsor):**

. . . .

. . . .

. . . .

. . . .

5. **Self-excluded at casinos or online?**

Yes ○   No ○

Which ones?

. . . .

For how long?

. . . .

Other comments:

. . . .

. . . .

. . . .

. . . .

Legal history:

. . . .

. . . .

. . . .

. . . .

Spiritual/religious preference:

. . . .

. . . .

. . . .

. . . .

SUMMARY AND TREATMENT

	Diagnosis	Code
AXIS I	1:	. . . .
	2:	. . . .

*

TREATMENT CONSIDERATIONS

Is the patient appropriate for outpatient treatment?   Yes ○   No ○

If no, explain and indicate referral made: . . . .

. . . .

. . . .

. . . .

TREATMENT PROGRAMS AND FREQUENCY RECOMMENDED

○ Individual   ○ Couples   ○ Family   ○ Gender-specific group

Summary of all initial treatment recommendations, including support groups, psychiatry evaluation, professional services (legal, financial), and self-exclusion:

. . . .

. . . .

. . . .

. . . .

. . . .

. . . .

Therapist's signature/credentials: . . . .

Date: . . . .

CHAPTER 6

HARM-REDUCTION APPROACHES ACROSS THE CONTINUUM

"All choices must reduce harm, not increase harm."

Following initial assessment, therapists have an ethical obligation to first do no harm regardless of clinical affiliation or credential (e.g., licensed clinical social worker, licensed clinical psychologist, marriage and family therapist, licensed practicing counselor, etc.). Adhering to the ethical value of "do no harm" is typically commonplace for practicing therapists. But when treating individuals struggling with an addiction, sometimes clinical judgment of "harm" doesn't match with the client's view of "harm" and the recommended course of treatment is mismatched.

A dictionary definition of "harm" is physical or mental damage (Merriam-Webster.com, 2019). Therefore, on the continuum of treatment options for addiction, it is reasonable that anything that produces "harm" to the client therefore constitutes "doing harm." Abstinence-based treatment tools such as self-exclusion and financial planning appear to provide the least amount of harm to the client. For instance, in abstinence-based treatments, gamblers are "not allowed" to gamble, which provides the least amount of harm to the client (i.e., no gamble, no harm), on the surface anyway.

On the other end of the treatment continuum, emerging new treatment approaches have sought to develop strategies to help reduce as much harm as possible while meeting the client where they are at in accepting help. Harm-reduction approaches provide clients with specified boundaries for substance or activity use, to establish safe use and minimize harm. While emerging evidence on harm-reduction strategies has been promising to date, there are limited resources available for therapists to understand what harm-reduction strategies are (and what they are not) and how to apply them in their work with their clients. As such, the current chapter seeks to provide an overview of harm-reduction strategies, generally and specifically related to gambling. Harm reducation incorporates everything from education about responsible gambling to total abstinence. It is the continuum of care for gambling addiction treatment.

Harm Reduction to Self-Exclusion: A Shared Continuum

Harm reduction has no agreed upon definition, and typically refers to an array of policies, programs, and strategies to reduce negative consequences related to gambling and other substance use (legal or illegal). Harm-reduction strategies impact individuals and communities through public health strategies aimed at helping the consumer or user, and in policies requiring the gambling industry to facilitate more harm-reduction strategies to promote safer play. Given the loose definition of harm reduction, and the breadth of philosophical and practical applications of strategies and approaches, it is important to consider the various aspects of harm reduction and how to use harm-reduction strategies in gambling treatment.

Harm reduction *is not* controlled gambling, a replacement or alternative to abstinence, for use with only one age group or gender, or for use when all else fails. At its core, harm reduction identifies ways in which individuals reduce harmful decisions or behaviors. The target is that every decision a person makes *must* reduce harm. Ultimately with harm reduction, the goal is abstinence, just not right away. As an alternative to the disease model perspective, harm-reduction strategies provide a more genuine therapeutic alliance between the therapist and the client, early in the clinical relationship and throughout the relationship. Harm reduction is a safety net for clients.

It is more than "allowing them to gamble"; it is about helping them see how much of their life they miss out on when they gamble to excess (or increase harm).

Harm-reduction strategies in therapy can allow for an open and non-judgmental space for the client to discuss their gambling and other harmful behaviors or decisions in their life. Taking this stance allows the client to develop a plan that they will actually believe in and report back to the therapist in future sessions.

Most therapists do not know or understand the definition of "harm reduction." Often, trainees make disapproving faces, their body language changes, and they make sarcastic comments about "controlled" drinking or using when asked about harm reduction. Unfortunately, these beliefs couldn't be further from the definition and the practical implementation known as harm reduction. Many therapists struggle with harm reduction, particularly if they are in recovery themselves (e.g., limiting their drinking or drug use didn't work for them, so why would it work for someone else?). Many therapists from various training disciplines or modalities may also struggle with harm reduction, particularly if their philosophy on addiction treatment leans towards total abstinence as the only way to stop the addiction (e.g., if their mentor didn't agree with harm reduction, the student won't have had any experience or exposure to using it in their clinical practice; many drug and alcohol treatment settings are abstinence-based). This stance assumes that all clients are addicted by the time they seek help. In fact, many clients seek help at a time in their life when they are making harmful choices and don't know what else to do on their own. Utilizing harm-reduction strategies can help clients gain self-awareness of their ability to set limits, self-regulate, control, and gain insight into their gambling behaviors.

Using Harm Reduction with Clients

Therapists must embrace harm reduction with every gambling client they meet. Again, it is not an approach to use when all else fails. It should be used from the beginning. A harm-reduction approach creates a supportive, non-judgmental relationship between the therapist and client. The client is given options, but will make their own choices. The therapist can educate around potential harm or risk, yet will still let the client determine their plan. This is where most therapists get tripped up. The key to making this approach successful is that the harm-reduction plan is continuously revisited and modifications are made until the harm-reduction plan reduces harm for the client. You can't create a plan with the client, review it once, and then say, "Well, there you have it! You can't gamble safely so let's talk about abstaining now." You must take a curious, supportive stance in reviewing which aspects of the harm-reduction plan worked and where it didn't work, showing a willingness to make slight adjustments until the overall plan works for the client. The therapist's stance is *against harm*, not against gambling, so you are in favor of any positive choices as defined by the client. All choices must reduce harm, not increase harm.

Best practice for using harm-reduction strategies is to focus on short-term goals and very targeted behavioral characteristics common in gambling. Examples of goals may include reducing the amount of time or money spent gambling while increasing other activities (visiting family/friends, reading, attending church). In some cases, it can take up to a year for someone to know whether they want/need to abstain from gambling, but it should always be their choice, not that of the therapist.

The 10 Rules of Responsible Gambling is the best guide to use with clients. It allows you to walk through each of the rules as you develop a harm-reduction plan for that client. All ten rules need to be addressed in some capacity as part of the overall harm reduction plan. Then the client will demonstrate self-control and self-regulation by following the plan. Using a blank sheet of paper with the client, you develop a plan that the client co-creates and is motivated to follow since you aren't taking the gambling completely away from them. Draw a large box on a blank sheet of paper. Consider giving an example that your client can relate to as you introduce the concept of a harm-reduction plan. For example, discuss what a playpen is used for with toddlers (play with minimal adult supervision without getting hurt). Then refer back to the box and say: "This is your playpen. Anything inside the box is what you can do. The goal is to not go outside the box as that will increase harm, not reduce harm, with every decision you make regarding your gambling." Then discuss each of the ten rules, creating specific rules to follow inside the box. You must follow all the rules, all the time, for this to be effective. You cannot select just a few rules as an effective harm-reduction plan. Make sure to actively discuss this with your clients.

10 Rules of Responsible Gambling

1. If You Choose to Gamble, Do So for Entertainment Purposes

Provide education to the client about this. Gambling is but one type of entertainment. Get them to identify other types of entertainment. Look for how they spend or used to spend their time, such as movies, dining, concerts, cultural events, hiking, walks, etc. If they are struggling to identify other types of entertainment, help them explore and expand as part of reducing harm. Get them to remember when gambling was fun and enjoyable as opposed to how it was when they felt compelled to gamble. As part of their plan, get them to commit to another entertainment activity during a given week.

2. Treat the Money You Lose as the Cost of Your Entertainment

Provide education about how we, as people, don't expect to get our money back at the end of a movie, dinner, or musical event. So why are we expecting to have more money after gambling than when we started? This is the cost of their entertainment. This discussion will lead into the next two rules. If you can, have your casino clients retrieve their latest win/loss report at the casino. This is a real eye-opener for many as they don't realize how expensive gambling has been for them. Some sports betting apps will have *reality checks* that can send a reminder of how much was wagered since logging in, but it may not give a monthly or yearly report, depending on the laws and jurisdiction.

3. Set a Dollar Limit and Stick to It

Allow the client to start the conversation about how much they can afford to "lose" gambling. Then help them dig into the details and include their current financial situation. Make sure not to sound judgmental or condescending when they want to spend more money than they actually have. And don't let countertransference show up, as you may never want to spend as much money as they would on gambling or any other activity for that matter.

Discuss how much they will spend during each gambling event (e.g., casino visit, sports betting on teams, buying lottery tickets or scratch-offs) and help them to do the math correctly. For example, a client wants to spend $500 when going to the casino. Then clarify if that is $500 per casino trip, or per week or per month. Often they will give a dollar amount without clarifying how much for each instance of gambling. Another example: $500 for football but there are eight games over the weekend. Is that $500 per bet ($4000) or $500 total ($62.50 per bet per team). When you get curious with the client, you both learn more about their current gambling behavior and can help the client to see how it was increasing harm and not reducing harm. Write the specific amount inside the box with qualifiers (per day, per game, per ticket).

4. Set a Time Limit and Stick to It

For many gamblers, they lose track of time while gambling. The idea of leaving when you have reached your time limit is a foreign concept. They only know to leave when the money is all gone. Have a conversation about how much time is reasonable—reinforcing that each decision needs to reduce harm, not increase harm. If they want to gamble for six hours, agree to it and discuss how they will know when the six hours is up. Will they set a reminder on their phone/watch? What if they spend their gambling budget before the six hours is reached? Remind them that every decision needs to reduce harm, so then they must go home early.

5. Expect to Lose

The house wins in the end. The bookie never goes bankrupt. The lottery continues to have drawings. Help the client to realize that gambling is entertainment, losing is the cost of their entertainment, and they should not expect to go home with more money.

6. Make It a Private Rule Not to Gamble on Credit

This requires some discussion because it means talking about more than just credit cards. For casino gamblers, get curious about whether they have taken cash advances to provide more money to gamble. Many sports betters create virtual pay accounts like Venmo and PayPal and attach credit cards to the account. If they must pay the bookie, these sites will draw from the cash advance line of credit on the credit cards. And others will begin to pay all their bills (i.e., groceries, utilities, gas) with a credit card so they have cash from their bank to gamble with. Exploring all these access points will help educate the client about choices to make that reduce harm as opposed to continue to increase harm. A harm-reduction plan cannot include the use of credit cards as that increases harm. Discussing this rule can oftentimes lead to revisiting Rule 3 to establish (and perhaps re-establish) a dollar limit.

7. Create Balance in Your Life

Clients need to review a typical week and identify activities that do not involve gambling—Sunday dinners with family, a niece/nephew/grand-child's school or afterschool event, exercise, family night, etc. Gambling often takes over many activities that were once a weekly occurrence, and sometimes clients are unsure where to start getting those things back. Help clients to return to these activities to be well rounded. Show a picture of an elephant balanced on a beach ball and ask clients if they have this level of balance. We can all strive for that balance. Write the activities that the client will do as part of the plan.

8. Avoid "Chasing" Lost Money

Educate the client about the DSM-5 (American Psychiatric Association, 2013) criteria for Gambling Disorder that specially identifies "chasing one's losses." If they answer "yes" to this question during the evaluation, then it isn't reducing harm. Again, the gaming industry will win in the end and chasing only means the client will lose more. By sticking to a dollar limit and time limit, and treating the money lost as the cost of entertainment, chasing losses can be avoided. Spend time to carefully craft a detailed plan so that the client understands how not to chase.

9. Don't Gamble as a Way to Cope with Emotional or Physical Pain

Many people will gamble when they have emotional pain, such as depression or grief. The act of gambling makes them feel better and they make the association "When I gamble, I feel better. I'm going to gamble again the next time I feel like this." The association between the dopamine surge and their verbal rule of "gamble again next time I feel like this" can create the urge to gamble even sooner in order to feel better.

When working with older adults or people with physical illnesses or disabilities, talk about how gambling helps them dissociate from their physical pain. They still have the pain, but they don't feel it while gambling. It creates an illusion that "when I gamble, I don't have back pain or hip pain. I'm going to do this more often. It feels good." Help the client to see that attending therapy on a regular basis reduces harm just as going to the doctor or specialist for regular check-ups reduces harm.

10. Become Educated about the Warning Signs of Problem Gambling

Following a well-constructed harm-reduction plan is one way to be educated about the warning signs. Spend time asking the client about their warning signs. How will they know if they are increasing harm instead of reducing harm with a decision? You will often hear about the dollar limit, time limit, or chasing for excitement. Maybe it is leaving the house at 12:01am because that is technically a "new day." Or they will postpone mailing a bill or change the payment date on their online banking website.

Caution: Make sure you help your client discuss harm reduction with their family members and loved ones. Most family members simply want them to stop/abstain and won't understand the effectiveness of a harm-reduction plan. Get a release of information to discuss directly with loved ones and answer their questions. Reiterate that abstinence is the goal, just not right away, and implementing a harm-reduction plan will keep the client engaged in therapy.

Over time, you and your client will make changes to the harm-reduction plan until it works and the client is confident in gambling responsibly. Because gambling, and addiction in general, is so much about control, implementing a harm-reduction plan gives your clients new ways of controlling aspects of their own lives in an impactful and meaningful way. Abstinence may be the ultimate goal of harm reduction, and over time as clients begin to fill their lives with other meaningful activities with friends and family, gambling will become less important.

Using Harm Reduction with Specific Populations

There are common themes across age groups, types of gambling, and sub-populations when using harm-reduction strategies. Harm-reduction plans must include setting limits, breaks in play, and increasing self-awareness about current gambling behavior. Setting limits includes money spent and time spent gambling. Breaks in play include taking breaks while at a gambling venue and not gambling every day. Increasing self-awareness includes not chasing losses, creating balance with other activities, not using credit, and not gambling as a way of escaping emotional or physical pain.

For *online gambling*, help clients create ways to set limits either within the gambling website or on their own. Examples of setting limits can include setting daily, weekly, or monthly limits on how much money is allowed to be deposited (within the gambling site) or connecting the gambling site to a specific bank account/card that only has limited funds available. Clients can set timers on their phone, computer, or household appliance (e.g., egg timer) to remind them when the time limit has been reached. To create breaks in play while gambling, the timer is used. Clients can put calendar appointments on their phone, email, or paper calendar to signal days they can gamble and days they cannot gamble. To increase self-awareness of current gambling behavior, request that the client journal is completed at the end of a gambling episode to capture how they are feeling (agitated, excited, depressed, etc.), whether they have urges to break the harm-reduction plan and keep gambling, whether they are thinking of ways to get more money to gamble, and any other clinically relevant information that can be discussed during therapy. Journaling is a great way to help bring reality of the gambling activity to the forefront of the client's mind. Some software sites may offer a "cool-off" period of responsible gambling where you select the number of days to be locked out of the site for time to cool off. All of these methods are self-directed by the individual. While these methods may not seem impactful, remember that creating an entire harm-reduction plan is the key to success, not just targeting one behavior. Unfortunately, strategies employed as responsible gaming initiatives implemented by the gambling operators only offer moderate decreases in harmful gambling behaviors (Harris & Griffiths, 2016; see also Chapter 1: Gambling Is Everywhere for overview of responsible gambling strategies). As such, therapists must help clients solve their own problems and select choices that reduce harm.

For *sports gambling,* many of the same rules apply as with online gambling and online sports gambling. Setting limits, creating breaks in play, and increasing self-awareness are key. Develop a plan that incorporates the type of sports (football, baseball, basketball, soccer) and the frequency of the games. Consider the buddy system where betting cannot occur alone or in isolation. The plan needs to target access, availability, frequency, and quantity, while increasing participation in non-gambling activities. Help your clients find ways to still engage in activities that feed their competitive desire and deal with boredom without gambling.

For *adolescents,* developing a harm-reduction plan can be tricky given that the legal age for gambling may be older than the adolescent. Adolescents live in a world where gambling is everywhere and becoming more socially acceptable every day. It is important to implement a plan that teaches making choices that reduce harm, not increase harm. Most common approaches focus on educating about gambling, dispelling myths about skill vs. luck, and addressing other distorted thinking patterns.

For *young adults,* the primary goal is to help them launch into adulthood successfully. This includes all aspects of their life—not just employment and independent living, but also dating and eventually coupling up. Introduce the concept of "natural recovery," helping to explain why more adolescents meet criteria for problem gambling, but the same number doesn't occur in adulthood. Many young adults abandon problematic gambling activities when life takes over (college/career, dating, building their own family, etc.). This is similar to excessive and binge drinking. Most young adults learn to drink more responsibly as they mature, which is also explained by the brain being fully developed at age 25.

For older adults, it can be complicated because, as therapists, we want to respect their right to self-determination and autonomy while also helping them to live within their financial means. Many adult children are concerned about their parent's gambling behavior but don't know how to talk about the gambling or money without sounding like roles have become reversed between parent and child. Depending on the age of the older adult, the stigma for seeking professional help is great and can also be a barrier. When you get to work directly with older adults and their gambling, it is important to implement a harm-reduction approach where they maintain control over the decisions and details of the plan. Creating a non-judgmental environment will help them to share if they could stay within the harm-reduction plan or not. Provide education in a variety of areas, allowing them to learn, talk about, and gain a sense of increased knowledge. The main areas include medications that have side effects, how to cope with grief and loss, money management, and having a sense of meaning and purpose ("What gets you up in the morning?").

For clients involved in the legal system due to their gambling, there is no choice but to abstain from gambling. Even though a client may want to continue to gamble, and we have just illustrated how to create a harm-reduction plan, clients involved in the legal system have marginalized choices. Tell your clients that you are not above the law; therefore, abstinence is the only treatment goal (see Chapter 10: The Legal System and Gambling for more information).

Self-Exclusion as Harm Reduction

Some clients will realize that they cannot gamble responsibly and abstinence is the main treatment goal. As discussed in Chapter 1: Gambling Is Everywhere, self-exclusion programs (voluntary exclusion programs) are one way to reduce harm on the opposite end of the harm-reduction continuum. Self-exclusion programs are one of the most widely used strategies for responsible gambling initiatives across many countries. Researchers (Blaszczynski, Ladouceur, & Nower, 2007; Blaszczynski *et al.*, 2011) measure self-exclusion as a harm-reduction intervention, from policy- and industry- to individual-level effectiveness. Researchers also believe that self-exclusion programs can be a gateway to treatment (Blaszczynski *et al.*, 2007). The design and implementation of this gateway path varies by country and operator but all maintain the same philosophy: Self-exclusion is a strategy for assisting problem gamblers by limiting their access and opportunities to gamble at their establishments. The clinical field acknowledges self-exclusion as an intervention for individuals to reduce or prevent access and opportunities to gamble (closing a door). Both arrive at the same outcome of preventing access as a way of reducing harm to individuals. The individual takes the initiative to self-exclude. In other words, the gaming industry doesn't approach individuals and enroll them into the self-exclusion program—hence the "self" in the name.

Self-exclusion programs are voluntary programs to exclude identified individuals from casinos or other gambling venues as a way of managing problematic gambling behavior. These programs vary from state to state and country to country, so it's important to become knowledgable about the specifics of these programs where you practice. Learn the time limits (six months, one year, five years, lifetime), where to sign up (at the location, government office, online website), and where else it will apply (some operators have a global presence). In the US, it is important that clients understand it is not the operator's job to keep them out—it is the client's responsibility to not enter. Self-exclusion programs are considered legal agreements, with penalties for self-excluders who violate the agreement up to and including trespassing. If a client enters after signing up for self-exclusion, they are increasing harm with their choices, not reducing harm.

With the increase of online gambling, many operators have developed self-exclusion programs for their online sites. This again will vary from state to state and country to country, and even operator to operator. The limitation with self-exclusion programs for online gambling sites is that the individual must self-exclude with every site and operator. The other limitation is that most online sites require that you sign up for their site first, before you can go through the procedure of self-excluding. While this may work for clients who already have accounts established, it doesn't make sense for them to sign up for new sites to then self-exclude. Technology companies have entered this space to help manage exclusion from online gambling sites by installing software on computers and handheld devices preventing access to any gambling websites, now and in the future. At the time of this publication, companies such as Gamblock and Gamban have developed commercial software solutions for self-excluding on gambling websites and apps.

When helping your clients who are choosing abstinence, self-exclusion programs are excellent ways to close some of the doors to gambling access. While no self-exclusion program or software will be 100% effective, they help put distance between the impulsive thought and the ability to act on it.

Conclusion

Harm-reduction plans are one of more important treatment aspects to addressing problematic and disordered gambling in individuals. Incorporating the stages of change model, motivational interviewing, and psycho-education about gambling in today's society, clients are more likely to develop a strong therapeutic alliance with you. This alliance and judgment-free environment will decrease the need to have a power and control battle. Utilizing a harm-reduction approach with your clients is a critical determining factor of their ability and willingness to keep coming to treatment. It is also critical in identifying successful strategies for closing doors to problematic gambling. Remember the continuum from 1) reducing harm with every choice to gamble, to 2) self-excluding from all sites and brick-and-mortar locations. Take the time to develop carefully tailored and effective harm-reduction strategies with your clients using the 10 Rules of Responsible Gambling. Review their plans during every session and help your clients solve ways to stick to their plans. At times when clients cannot stick to their harm-reduction plan, help them move to abstinence with buy-in and internal motivation.

Case Examples of Harm Reduction on a Continuum

The following cases illustrate how to design a harm-reduction plan for specific clients. The first case illustrates how to implement self-exclusion as a harm-reduction strategy for those who want to abstain from gambling completely. The second case illustrates how to implement self-exclusion initially, due to idiosyncratic client contextual factors. In Dave's case, the illustration showcases how self-exclusion programs will automatically cancel players' club memberships. This is important because getting special offers and freeplay notices by mail or email is an invitation to return to the gambling establishment, which is a violation. Cases use client pseudonyms and details are omitted or altered to protect client confidentiality.

Case 1: Marty

Marty is an 81-year-old widowed female, seeking help for her gambling problem. Her daughter and son-in-law recently told her that they were worried about the amount of money she was withdrawing from the ATM while at the casino. She enjoys playing the slots and is a member of the casino's player club; she also enjoys the buffet breakfast, where she can use her player's card to eat for free.

Together, Marty and her therapist developed a harm-reduction plan for her to follow. It consisted of the following rules, plus education for Rules 1, 9 and 10:

- Rules 2, 3, and 5: Her budget is $500/week, or $2,000/month, and no more than $24,000/year. This was verified by her daughter and son-in-law as within budget.
- Rule 4: She cannot go to the casino two days in a row. This includes two consecutive days over two weeks. She originally wanted to go on a Saturday and Sunday and considered it two different weeks.
- Rule 4: She cannot stay longer than three hours; she must get up and walk around, and get something to eat and/or drink at the two-hour mark.
- Rules 6 and 8: She cannot use the ATM machine at the casino and she must leave her debit and credit cards at home.
- Rule 5: If she spends her $500 before the three hours are up, she must go home. If she has money left over at the three-hour mark, she also must go home. She cannot return to the casino even to get at the buffet once she has hit the three-hour mark.
- Rule 7: She will only eat at the buffet three times a week. She will schedule time with friends, over lunch or dinner, during the week as part of her

balanced entertainment activities. Or she will sign up for some activity at the local community center.

- She can call the therapist after a day of gambling and leave a voicemail about how she did following her harm-reduction plan. This will help her remember what to share before too much time has passed.

Case 2: Dave

Dave is a 29-year-old single male, who lives with parents due to excessively gambling at casinos. He seeks help at the request of his parents. After completing a thorough financial inventory and financial restitution plan, the client agrees that self-exclusion would be helpful for him for several reasons. He wants to show his parents that he is taking this seriously and he wants to tell his friends that he can't go to the casino as he could be arrested for trespassing (his way of handling peer pressure). In his state of residence, the self-exclusion program offers one- and five-year terms, as well as lifetime. The therapist discusses signing up for one year, as five years seems too difficult to conceptualize at his age. He schedules an appointment at the local government office, signs up, and provides his parents with proof. He shares in his next therapy session that a "huge weight has been lifted" and discusses how the threat of being arrested for trespassing is helpful when he has urges or cravings as well as when his friends pressure him to go with them to the casino.

CHAPTER 7

FINANCES

"Money is supposed to hurt when you spend it."

Understanding the finances of your client is one of the most critical components of effective treatment for disordered gambling. Over the years, many therapists have told us that they are uncomfortable discussing and providing suggestions to their clients about their finances and financial situation, mostly due to their own insecurities and perceived inadequate financial situations. In her book *Women and Money*, Suze Orman (2010) says that we are more comfortable talking about our deepest secrets than we are about money—even with our closest friends. This is a real issue in today's society, and therapists must work towards becoming confident in discussing personal financial matters when treating problem gamblers.

As competent therapists, you need to work through any countertransference issues related to money as problem gambling treatment requires a thorough financial strategy that is created early in the treatment relationship and monitored frequently. Understanding and working with your client's finances requires interventions to reduce access to money (i.e., *close all the doors* for the client), develop a budget that includes restitution (or repayment plan), and establish an accountability system for responsibility and oversight.

You will need to help implement some immediate strategies to target finances from the beginning of treatment, in order to *close all the doors* that lead towards gambling. These immediate strategies include 1) limiting access to money via bank debit cards, 2) no longer borrowing from family and friends, and 3) no longer taking loans, such as payday loans, casino line of credit, or cash advances on credit cards. Identifying these immediate actions gives you time to develop a budget and repayment plan (i.e., restitution) which can take several weeks or months. Consider all the ways your client accesses money such as debit/credit cards, bank checks, money apps, and cash, to work towards *closing the doors* and limiting access while increasing accountability.

Real Money and Gambling Money

For most people, there is "money." For gamblers, there is "real" money and "gambling" money. Real money is used to pay bills, buy food, and meet other household expenses. Gambling money is used for gambling. These two buckets of money do not intersect until there isn't enough gambling money to gamble with. Then real money is used for gambling. However, if there isn't enough real money to pay the bills, a gambler will not consider using the gambling money to pay for these things. Gambling money is only for gambling.

This may sound ridiculous, but when you have this discussion with your clients, they will completely agree with the concept of real and gambling money as separate and never to intersect. Try it and you will see! You will need to help your clients understand that there is only money, and if there isn't enough money to pay for food, shelter, and other necessities, then there isn't enough money for gambling. This is especially important when creating a harm-reduction plan. It also creates a natural opportunity to talk more about their current employment situation and whether they need to consider working full-time or getting a part-time job in addition to their current work to begin paying their debts.

Why Bankruptcy Is Not an Option

The term "bailout" was not well understood by the general population until the US economic crash of 2008. Since then, many associate bailouts with the car industry, housing markets, and even banking. Bailouts are one of the criteria for Gambling Disorder. Bailouts are viewed as a fast way back to gambling. They remove the pressure, the consequences, and the negative feelings of gambling to excess and causing financial problems.

Gamblers Anonymous (GA) views bankruptcy as a form of bailout. The NORC (National Opinion Research Center, 1999) found that over 10% of problem gamblers and over 19% of pathological gamblers have declared bankruptcy, compared to only 4% of non-gamblers. This implies that, in the early 2000s, individuals who met criteria for a gambling disorder were five times more likely to declare bankruptcy. When people file bankruptcy, it removes them from the financial responsibility of paying back the debt they incurred. Anyone, but in particular those with a gambling disorder, need to be reminded frequently that the debt is due to the consequences of their lack of responsibility and accountability. Bankruptcy laws have changed in recent years and it is more difficult to qualify for bankruptcy. Nonetheless, having a conversation about wanting a "quick fix" or impulsively getting rid of debt caused by gambling can be tied to their gambling beliefs. Many believe that all it takes is one win, and all their problems are solved. Whether it is a jackpot with the lottery, March Madness tournament, Super Bowl win, or progressive slots jackpot, a big win will take away all debt (quickly) and all their problems are solved. Bankruptcy fits with this "win" of removing the consequences caused by gambling and other impulsive spending behaviors.

Explore other high-risk situations with your clients and help to problem-solve or role-play how to handle these situations. For example, the bookie texts that he will give your client an opportunity to bet on the Sunday game, even though your client owes the bookie a lot of money already. Role-play how to say "no" or just not respond to the text message or even delete the bookie from contacts. Discuss the distorted thinking of this high-risk situation. For instance, your client may share the distorted thought "If you place just one bet and win, then you will repay the bookie and that problem will be solved." However, there is a higher probability the client will lose and owe even more money.

Money Protection

In training, therapists talk extensively about protecting the client from themselves as well as helping the family/spouse/partner have protection moving forward. These concepts require confidence on your part. You want to help your clients create distance between an impulsive thought and the ability to act on it, regardless of whether they have a harm-reduction or total abstinence plan. Explore all the possible "doors" that need to be closed in order to reduce and/or prevent continued access to money for problematic gambling. Explore solutions that may be viewed as short-term as opposed to lifelong by your client—for instance, removing their name from debit/credit cards and bank accounts; having a spouse/partner open a separate bank account without the client's name and take over all bill paying for the household. Depending on the situation, remove valuable possessions from the home that could be sold or pawned for gambling money, even if only temporarily.

When a client has caused extensive financial damage as a result of their gambling, we discuss strategies such as alerting the credit reporting agencies to stop soliciting (e.g., Opt Out Prescreen[1]), accessing their credit report to determine how many accounts exist,[2] or changing the daily withdrawal limit amount on a debit card or removing cash advances on credit cards. Some may need to have their paycheck automatically deposited into a separate account or tell family/friends not to loan them any more money.

As you work through the finances with your client, help them to understand how "control" plays a significant part in their disordered gambling. So much about problematic gambling is about control. You may say to your client: "As you move to having a better relationship with money, in what ways are you still trying to control things you don't have control over?" A common situation involves when and how much to pay as part of the repayment plan. Many clients will negotiate whether that debt should be paid at this time, or if the payment amount per month should be honored at all. As you investigate more about their financial mindset, you begin to see how they control how much they need to be accountable and responsible. For instance, often clients will say to us: "When you are already maxed out on your credit cards, what

1   www.optoutprescreen.com
2   www.annualcreditreport.com/index.action

does it matter if you pay this month or next month as you can't use the card right now anyways."

This is the distorted and unhealthy relationship with money and debt that problematic gambling fosters. A client once asked if he should pay his car insurance this month or get his car inspected? When asked more questions, he revealed that the car was past due for inspection but he was four months behind on his car payments and received a repossession notice. His logic about repayment was completely disrupted since he wasn't going to have the car much longer, yet he was focused on the insurance for the car. These are situations that you will need to help your clients problem-solve, and you can only get there by having regular discussions about money and debt repayment. Make the conversation about money a part of every session. Show your clients that talking about finances is part of recovery, and recovery has accountability and responsibility.

Financial Inventory for Restitution Plan

Clarifying Debt and Expenses

It is important to introduce the topic of money and finances early in the thera-peutic relationship. Think of it as educating your clients about having a healthy relationship with money. As part of your gambling evaluation, you will want to ask about how much they are spending on gambling, whom they owe due to gambling, whether they have declared bankruptcy in the past, and if they are currently using any outside supports such as the food bank, church donations, or utility assistance. Then move to a more thorough inventory of their finances. This may take a few sessions as many do not know how much they owe as part of their avoidant coping strategy. Many report not opening their mail or just throwing the bills away without paying them. Gamblers Anonymous (GA) 12-Step fellowship includes a step on financial responsibility (Step 4: Made a searching and fearless moral and *financial* inventory of ourselves). Other 12-Step fellowships, such as AA or NA, do not include "and financial" in Step 4.

Begin to capture your client's income (either net pay or monthly) and expenses. Some find it helpful to have a list of expense categories. The overall goal is to capture all the expenses that occur monthly (e.g., rent/mortgage, utilities, phone, food, gas for transportation, etc.). Then capture the sources of debt such as credit cards, family/friends, bank loans, bookie, co-workers, neighbors, etc. Make sure to include the total amount owed, interest fee, and current monthly payment (often the minimum payment). You may decide to give this as homework or it may be better addressed during the session. Depending on the age of your client, consider creating a shared document (e.g., shared Google Sheet) to create the financial inventory with your client. Then you can share the sheet and your client can fill in the details outside of the session. You can open it during future sessions to add more details.

Once you have this information, you can begin to create a budget and restitution plan. If your client wants to continue to gamble, this is where the cost of entertainment fits as part of the harm-reduction plan. It can also be used to determine if they can afford to gamble at all, based on the outcome of this exercise. It's common to have more expenses than income. A gambler's mind might exclude the debt owed to people as a way of justifying having fewer expenses. Once you include the gambling debt, many do not have enough income to support continued gambling. Let the numbers tell the story so you can stay aligned with your client.

Debt Repayment/Financial Restitution Plan

Clients often do not consider paying some of their debt, particularly to friends/family. When they borrow a large sum of money, such as $5000, many hold the mindset that when they have that large sum of money ($5000), then (and only then) they will pay the loan back. You need to help them understand that having a large sum of money rarely happens when money is viewed as money rather than real vs. gambling money. You need to help them break down all their debt into manageable monthly payments. Yes, this may sound simple, but many gambling-disordered individuals have such a terrible relationship with money that all these concepts are new to them. Factor some of the co-occurring bio-neurological, psychological, or socio-cultural factors into this, and your clients are uncomfortable making payments for 24–36 months or even ten years simply to pay off debt. It is imperative that all debts are paid every month, even if it is $5 repayment. The act of paying debts helps to reinforce that problematic gambling was the cause of this financial situation and it keeps the consequences in the forefront of the client's day-to-day life. You want to keep the accountability of restitution close to the client as you help them develop a healthier relationship with money. Consider using this phrase with your clients: "It's a universal principle that we can all spend more than we make. Money is supposed to hurt when we spend it."

The financial restitution plan is more than a monthly budget—it's a living financial plan with payoff amounts and dates as part of the plan. Work with your client to develop a plan that shows monthly payments and remaining balance every month after making a payment. Then extend the plan to show when the debt will be paid off. This level of detail is eye-opening and revealing for clients. It makes clients stand super close with the consequences of their gambling. Next, discuss how the gambler's mind would naturally want to gamble to win a large amount of money to quickly pay it, as opposed to having a 24–36-month timeframe to pay. Help to process their thinking and remind them that money is supposed to hurt when you spend it.

With a completed financial restitution plan, determine ways to monitor this plan over time with your client. Have clients bring their computer to an appointment and log into their bank account or use their smartphone app. Have a family member join a session periodically to review financial oversight and progress. Use the shared file with your client to revise the debt repayment plan as they make payments. Whatever it is, there needs to be constant reporting of progress. Failure to follow up in later sessions could result in a repayment plan that doesn't work and a risk of relapse.

Involving Family Member(s)

Involving family members (however family is defined) needs to be done carefully so that issues of power and control are not dysfunctional (see also Chapter 8: Family for additional information about involving families in gambling treatment). When possible, invite the family member into a session to further discuss the finances, elicit any additional information that can inform the plan, and discuss how to implement accountability into the restitution plan.

There are many ways to have family members/supporters be a part of the recovery process for your client. Make sure the family member understands not to pay off the gambling and other debts too quickly. Oftentimes, families have extreme anxiety over debt and want to find ways to pay it down or off quickly. This is also considered a bailout, and families need to be educated about not paying debt too quickly. Family involvement strategies can vary from extreme control to passive oversight. Extreme control is when the family/support person takes over all the bill paying, access to money, and daily oversight of how the client spends money, and is accountable for showing evidence of that spending. For instance, the client needs to show payment receipts for small transactions including parking meter fees, bus tickets, and lunch. There are some emerging online tools to assist in this level of daily monitoring. For example, prepaid Visa cards are available that show all transactions in an online portal.

On the other end, passive oversight can simply be having login access to the client's online banking portal, with permission to review all transactions. If the client knows the family member will see questionable transactions, they may resist the impulse to gamble or bet in the first place. Families are encouraged to question the transactions but not feel responsible for controlling or stopping their loved one from gambling. Help educate family members about power and control dynamics that may be unhealthy when they assume the passive oversight role and how to avoid playing into this dynamic. For example, role-play with a family member a discussion about a questionable transaction. Get them to ask for clarification in a non-leading way and share their own emotional experience when they saw the transaction in question.

Asset Protection Plan for Partner/Spouse and Children

This section is dedicated to helping the partner/spouse/family member as the client. You will use these strategies to protect your client from further damage from their loved one's gambling problem. Helping family members develop financial protection plans can be foreign to most therapists. Think of your training in developing safety plans for individuals in domestic violence/ intimate partner violence situations. Therapists are trained to teach clients (family members) how to keep themselves safe during a violent incident or current living situation; if they plan to leave their partner, how to stay safe in a new environment; safety at work with an employer; and whether they should obtain a protection-from-abuse order. Take these concepts and apply them to disordered gambling for the partner/spouse and family. Often, the family member is just learning of all the financial devastation that has occurred. You are helping to get them up to speed during a "crisis" time. Develop a *financial asset protection plan* that reviews all sources of income and assets that need to be protected from gambling. Explore with the family everything that the person with a gambling disorder could access, sell, or use to secure a loan and determine ways to prevent further access. Protection plans for family members should exist whether the person with a gambling problem is seeking help or is continuing to gamble. Discuss how much information should be shared with the loved one with a gambling problem; this may depend on whether that person is seeking help.

The *Personal Financial Strategies for the Loved Ones of Problem Gamblers Guide* (National Endowment for Financial Education, 2000) was originally published to help protect families and spouses from continued financial devastation caused by disordered gambling. It provided a roadmap for gaining control over sources of income, limiting exposure to debt, and shifting the ownership and financial oversight. There hasn't been a new or updated version of this guide, nor have there been any more recent guides developed, so it is recommended that therapists use it as a guide for conversations with families. You need to help family members close all the doors to protect themselves from future financial problems and identify theft. Therapists should also help family members as clients to determine the following actions to take:

- Open a new bank account in only their name; decide where to keep paper checks and debit card, and what to tell the bank (alerts).
- Manage all income coming to the household and determine how to pay bills and maintain food, shelter, and other necessities.
- Turn on identify theft protection, call credit agencies (Transunion, Equifax, etc.) and freeze new accounts from being opened.
- Review all 401K/retirement accounts, if they exist, including at work, and change passwords and mailing address if necessary.
- If the financial devastation is severe and the family member is

considering leaving the relationship, help them to seek legal counsel for further guidance. Many employers offer EAP services that include a 30-minute legal consultation for free or little expense.

- For those with more income, consider alerting the accountant, accounting firm, and/or financial advisors about the gambling problem.
- Review any assets that could be used to secure more loans, such as car titles, home equity line of credit (HELOC), or borrowing against 401K accounts.
- Discuss the financial protection plan with key family members.

As discussed, the protection plan should be designed to protect the family member from any further loans taken out against their name without their knowledge, in addition to protecting them from other ways to get credit without their consent.

Conclusion

Overall, finances are a major component to treating gambling disorders and need to be attended to early, often, and for as long as possible. Developing a peer consultation group of other trained therapists will make individual client case situations more manageable, approachable, and thorough. Each financial protection plan needs to be tailored to the individual and their situation. Consider developing worksheets or electronic files for every client to complete. Also learn about prepaid Visa cards and other services that can aid in the financial treatment for your clients. Develop a network of other therapists across your region, state, country, and the globe to keep sharing information and best practices in the gambling treatment community.

Case Examples for Implementing Finance Strategies

The following cases have been created from our clinical experience, to illustrate how to design and implement finance strategies for specific clients. The first case illustrates how to implement financial strategies with a client who is single, while the second case illustrates how to incorporate a significant other into financial strategies. Both cases highlight the importance of addressing debt during therapy, and each case provides a unique approach to debt resolution. Cases use client pseudonyms and details are omitted or altered to protect client confidentiality.

Case 1: Eva

Eva is a 41-year-old divorced woman seeking gambling counseling after several years of compulsive gambling. She had been in counseling before but had not been willing to work on a plan that involved her finances until now. Eva reported a history of cannabis (still uses periodically) and had five years of sobriety for alcohol, which she credits to AA. She wants help from the therapist to "surrender" her finances without losing independence and control as a woman. She states that Step 1 of admitting she was powerless has always been a struggle for her but understands she needs to do something about her access to her own money. Eva has a history of compulsive gambling on social gaming sites on her iPad, and sometimes goes to the local casino with her friends.

During her first session with the therapist, she had a handwritten list of the goals she wants to achieve while working together. The list included being able to purchase a new smartphone, new clothes, and new furniture. She also wanted to pay the people she owed due to gambling, and save money to visit her daughter, who was living in another country at the time. Eva and the therapist discussed the importance of adhering to a budget on a weekly basis as well as developing a plan to prevent her from accessing her own money. Over the next few sessions, they developed a financial budget that included her income and all expenses, including her payoff plan for gambling debts. The budget allowed her to have $125 every week to cover groceries, gas for her car, and lunch or a snack twice a week.

Her overall budget took into account her income and paid her mortgage, car payment, car insurance, cell phone, weekly allowance ($125), health insurance copays, credit card debts, and gambling debt. Eva and the therapist completed a spreadsheet that listed which bills would be paid with each paycheck (first or second day of the month). She scheduled all her bills through online payments through her banking website. She signed up for a prepaid Visa card, gave the credit and debit cards to her daughter to hold, and had her daughter change her online banking password so she no longer would have access.

Every session, Eva and her therapist would log into the prepaid Visa website and review her spending. The therapist would comment on any compulsive spending behaviors such as overspending at Target on a Wednesday night, to overspending at her favorite store at the mall on Saturday. They would use this financial review to provide education about living within her means, identifying urges to gamble when she was low on funds, and how she felt when she was able to pay her bills successfully without being late.

After nine months of this financial plan, Eva was able to pay off her credit card and gambling debts to family/friends. She then used the money to save up to buy a plane ticket to see her daughter. She went on to use that extra money to buy new clothes and updated furniture for her house.

Twelve months into therapy, Eva had reached some significant milestones. She requested that she keep using the prepaid Visa as it was the best form of accountability for her. She continued in therapy to work on her relationship with money long after she had one year clean from gambling. She credits her clean time to surrendering her finances in a way that preserved her rights as a single woman.

Case 2: Nick

Nick is a 34-year-old married male seeking gambling counseling after his wife discovered he borrowed $78,000 from his mother to cover his gambling debt. During the initial intake, Nick and his wife shared that he had kept his gambling a secret for 12 years and had been lying about it for their entire nine-year relationship. Nick's wife was extremely angry and required Nick to sign a postnuptial to prevent further financial devastation to the family. The therapist discussed all the financial strategies that they could implement. Nick's wife agreed to take over all the finances, open a bank account in her own name, and have the paychecks deposited into that account to pay the bills. Nick would have a weekly budget of $100 and his restitution would be $400/month. Nick would not have access to any bank accounts or other financial-related websites/logins. The restitution plan would take over 16 years to pay the gambling debt. His wife repeatedly wanted to make changes to the plan to pay it off sooner because having that much debt made her anxious, so the therapist provided education to the wife that paying debt off too soon could become a trigger to gambling again, and explained that Nick's recovery would benefit from having to make a monthly payment that reminded him of his gambling consequences.

Nick and his wife also discussed that he was employed as a realtor and received a commission on a somewhat regular basis but they never knew how much it would be until he received it. Nick initially wanted to have some of his commission check as spending money because he "earned" it, while his wife reported using it for vacations and upgrades to their house. His wife didn't know how to respond. The therapist suggested that all commission checks go towards debt regardless of the amount, and his wife agreed to put all commission checks towards gambling debts.

Nick also agreed to sign up for LifeLock and made his wife the primary contact person for any alerts to his credit or financial situation. His wife removed all financial paperwork from the house and used a credit reporting app to monitor credit activity on a regular basis.

CHAPTER 8

FAMILY

"Gambling affects not just the gambler, but the whole family."

Families can be defined differently depending upon culture or grouping of individuals, but a family is commonly considered to be a group of individuals who are connected with each other through genetic/biological, psychological, sociocultural history and the family unit's future together (McGoldrick, Gerson & Shellenberger, 1999). For the purposes of this chapter, we consider family as 1) your client, 2) support members to your client, 3) all family members actively participating in counseling, or 4) a combination of the above. Family members (however defined) have a significant impact on each other's overall functioning, development, quality of life, and wellbeing.

Family involvement can be complex as it relates to gambling and the treatment of gambling disorders. The role of family can positively or negatively impact individuals with a gambling disorder. As discussed in Chapter 2: Understanding Gambling Disorder, development of a gambling disorder is not only a result of genetics (Grant *et al.*, 2015), but also a result of psychosocial factors (Magoon and Ingersoll, 2006). Individuals with a gambling disorder can also impact family members and the relationship with family, even if other family members abstain from gambling. This topic of family can be extremely emotional and often frustrating when determining which interventions, at what time, will be most helpful.

Family Systems Theory Review

Working with individuals is often a linear process of determining a diagnosis, understanding internal processes (cognition and feelings), and attending to their individual experiences and perspectives. The goal is to help the individual change. When working with a family (system), therapists assess family processes and rules, family relationships and roles, and understand the family and community experiences. The goal is to change the system. The family system is greater than the sum of its individual members and performs specific functions, and the system has subsystems (parents, parent/ child, and siblings) and boundaries. Changes in any part of a subsystem change the entire system. For example, the family system includes parents and children. When one of the children goes off to college, the subsystem of siblings changes and the system itself is changed.

It is important to understand how symptoms are 1) viewed as an expression of dysfunction in the family, 2) serving the whole family, 3) functioning as a solution; not to mention 4) what would be happening if these symptoms did not exist. It is imperative to understand how problematic behaviors, such as excessive gambling, serve a purpose for the family, and how excessive gambling unintentionally helps to maintain the family process and symptomatic behaviors across generations, but it also serves as a function of the family's inability to operate productively. In understanding how symptoms serve the family functioning, therapists can determine how best to bring about change that will help the family system become more functional and healthy.

First and Second Order Change

First and Second Order Change is a concept that can assist therapists in evaluating what changes have occurred in the past and how it served the family. From this understanding, therapists will understand how to implement Second Order Change. Understanding First and Second Order Change will help to determine what interventions to implement, when, and how to implement them to create healthy change in the family system. These changes are directly related to the treatment of a gambling disorder. First Order Change is when something changes according to the current rules of the system. Second Order Change is when the rules themselves change and therefore the system has to change. Often, families will implement First Order Change strategies to impact the gambling on their own and ultimately experience frustration when the gambling behavior continues. We can help families determine how to change the rules of their system to have an impact on the gambling behaviors.

Let's take a closer look at this concept. The Nine-Dot Problem (Maier, 1930) is a great way to understand First and Second Order Change.

1   Draw nine dots on a piece of paper.

2   Connect all nine dots with four straight lines without lifting your pen/ pencil from the paper.

People often believe this exercise is difficult, if not impossible. This is because they are trying to solve the problem with a First Order Change.

1   Apply Second Order Change and go outside of the nine dot area.

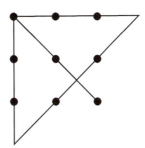

Now, apply this concept to your work with families. Take, for example, two parents who are very committed to helping their children in any way possible. They may feel guilty and even responsible because their adult child has a gambling problem. All they want to do is help. First Order Change: Parents give money to a young adult because of debt caused by excessive gambling. Parents are trying to help their young adult child hit "reset" and start over. Maybe if they help to remove the debt, the young adult will learn from the mistakes and move forward without gambling again. However, this does not change the rules of the system. It simply relieves the pressure of the consequences caused by gambling; it does not change the behavior of the young adult child moving forward. Call out the First Order Change rules that the parents keep following. Are they still following the rules of providing for their children, even though the child is an adult now? With Second Order Change, the parents require a budget and debt repayment plan, self-exclusion for one year, and access to a bank account to monitor spending activities before considering giving any financial help. This changes the rules of the system, requiring accountability and responsibility for the consequences caused by gambling. The young adult is now reminded of what excessive gambling caused every time he has to review his budget and payment plan with his parents.

When considering First and Second Order Change with clients, it is imperative to time the interventions with the family just right, because doing too much too soon can become a form of bailout for the entire family. This is most often a concern when working on the finances with the family. Clarify the family members' priorities, identify your priorities, and negotiate realistic goals that focus first on safety, then on closing "doors" accessed by the addiction, and ultimately on attending to the emotional needs of everyone.

Provide Education about Suicide

It is important to openly talk about suicide and help the family member determine what to do, if/when their loved one mentions or threatens suicide. First and foremost, help family members to know when to call 911 or the ambulance service, or where to take someone who openly talks about suicide (ER, local hospital). Review with the family if their loved one has a history of suicidal thoughts, plans, or attempts. Determine if there is imminent risk and if you need to take action as a professional. Provide local and/or national suicide helpline numbers to your client, encouraging them to program them into their phone as a contact, and discuss if their geographical region has any mobile crisis services they can call if needed.

Provide Education about Gambling Disorder

Take time to explain that gambling disorder is a biopsychosocial disorder that impacts their bio-neurological, psychological, and socio-cultural relationships (see also Chapter 2: Understanding Gambling Disorder). Explain how it is a mental health disorder, often characterized as an addiction, like drugs or alcohol, except the person doesn't ingest anything first before having compulsive or disordered behavior. People gamble for a wide range of different reasons, from bio-neurological or psychological to environmental reasons (such as how easy it is to access).

There can be a biological component to a gambling disorder that explains why some people gamble and others do not. The serotonin, noradrenergic, and dopamine deficits help to explain cognitive and emotional dysregulation, impulsivity, and reward deficits. These lead to gambling as a drug helping to focus, relieve stress, stabilize mood, and create euphoria that substitutes for satisfaction (see also Chapter 2: Understanding Gambling Disorder).

The psychosocial component can be explained by the familial environment and other social supports, loneliness, social disruption, bereavement and losses, work environment, social status, and social integration. Also considering trauma and abuse, chaos and neglect, and even over-indulgence in childhood and upbringing can contribute to the development of a gambling disorder. Issues with sense of self and self-object relations, core beliefs, and ego deficits help to explain how gambling creates a fantasy identity, a sense of escape as a solution, re-enacting trauma and loss with the illusion of gaining control as the outcome, and regulating mood or escaping from intolerable emotions.

Spiritual and religious settings often promote gambling as safe and something everyone can participate in without harm, so gambling is reinforced as an approved activity. On the other hand, individuals may have a crisis in their faith, experience spiritual abuse, or lack a spiritual life altogether. Having fear or rage at their God, misinterpreting luck as faith, an extreme sense of guilt and shame, and general lack of meaning contribute to anger, loneliness, alienation, lack of direction, and need to be favored by their God. Gambling then takes on a sense of purpose and meaning, which can help people escape from oppressive belief systems or escape and hide from their God. Gambling is proof of spiritual worth or unworthiness and luck is their higher power. Explore the family expectations regarding religion and spirituality, determining if there is a conflict between what the family believes and wants vs. what the individual with a gambling problem believes and wants. And if there is a conflict, help the family find a way to resolve the conflict or compromise with their loved one as part of recovery for all.

Cultural influences and contributors to gambling are vast and yet very individualized. Understanding ethnic, religious, and other cultural factors helps to explain gambling behaviours, including personal norms, beliefs, and values, and how they impact individual ideas and decisions. Annual rituals and celebrations may endorse gambling as a behavior that everyone engages in, safely and without consequences. Conversely, stigma related to asking for professional help can delay seeking help and utilizing community support and resources until the problem gambling is severe. Determine if, and in what ways, the family may be endorsing gambling without realizing the conflicting messages. Or is the family still encouraging gambling by inviting their loved one to events that would be triggers or past gambling places (e.g., football games, anniversary at the casino, etc.).

Discuss other addictive behaviors and how they may be interactional (e.g., drinking alcohol leads to gambling episode; excessively drinks after a gambling episode). Review any current or historical mental health disorders that may not be treated effectively, or are under-treated or under-diagnosed. Family can provide historical context that can assist in proper diagnosis and treatment.

Provide education about Gamblers Anonymous (GA) and Gam-anon and other self-support options. Explore faith and spiritual-based options (e.g., Celebrate Recovery®). See Chapter 9: Self-Help and Peer Supports for more information.

Discuss with family about setting limits and having to "detach with love," but still have an attachment since they are managing the finances. This concept is helpful but frustrating for families to understand. They need to learn to exercise the right amount of accountability without controlling their loved one's recovery program. Encourage family members to stay in therapy for themselves, even if/when things get better. When the crisis phase is over, help the family members to learn to focus on themselves and how they can grow and change too.

Family members will benefit from a longer therapeutic relationship after the crisis is over. This is where you can help sustain Second Order Change so that the system itself gets healthier. Encourage them to stay focused on themselves and work on codependency issues that exist in the relationship. When the entire system changes, the individuals also change and get better. Instill hope and optimism that making difficult choices now will ultimately help their loved one reduce excessive gambling or even abstain from gambling.

Whether it is the entire family, partners, or parents and children, the first few sessions need to focus on finances and suicidality. As part of your comprehensive evaluation, include a suicide risk assessment and complete a financial review (see Chapter 7: Finances for additional discussion).

Consider making a checklist that everyone completes and reviews periodically at the beginning of your sessions. Ultimately, therapists will help create a financial snapshot, monthly budget, and financial restitution plan. Help everyone to develop healthy accountability, monitor chronic control dynamics, and make sure everyone is involved in the financial details on a regular basis.

As therapists move into the next phase of therapy, issues related to communication and expressing feelings, control vs. involvement, and understanding accountability and responsibility will be key therapy goals and objectives. Teach effective communication skills and help the family begin to share feelings and express difficult emotions so the healing can begin. Family members need help expressing their trust issues, disbelief in the lies and secrecy, and sadness related to the gambler's behaviors. Oftentimes, the family member is playing "catch up" with the gambler since the addiction was hidden for so long before coming to light. We must help the family effectively move from the past to the present here and now without minimizing their emotions and feelings. Yet we want to stay mindful of anger that can become toxic anger—where the family member holds the anger and uses it to keep distance, punish, criticize, or engage in any other negative forms of interacting, to keep from moving forward. Implementing Second Order Change may be an effective way to get everyone realigned and moving forward together.

Working with the Family: Spouse/Partner and Gambler

Couples counseling with gambling addiction is similar to couples counseling for other chemical and behavioral addictions. The "relationship" between partner and spouse is your client, *not* the individuals in the relationship themselves. Share this approach with the couple to help them understand your role in remaining unbiased and objective. According to Ciarrocchi (2001), there are three common family responses to the individual with a gambling disorder:

- *Family accepts* the individual with a gambling disorder with little loss of intimacy
- *Parallel existence*, where partner is emotionally cold, some level of interaction, appearance of unity, but has minimal expectations related to intimacy and accepts coexisting to protect self from any future devastations
- *Chronically angry*, where the family member remains in the relationship but with intense conflict, regardless of abstinence from gambling.

As part of a comprehensive couples evaluation, consider who has the power in the relationship and what are the reality-based needs (i.e., food, utilities, bills), and assess the perspectives of the couple with respect to the safety and care of their children. Identify intimacy-based needs that are currently unmet and determine the level of severity of trust and anger issues. Partners lose trust first; the individual with a gambling disorder wants to get trust back first; and the disconnect between "when trust will be restored" needs to be openly discussed in sessions.

Conduct the assessment, exploring the courtship history to better determine which of the three responses may be more likely a fit currently or will become so without professional intervention. Help the couple to externalize the gambling problem, giving it the name (i.e "*It*"), and re-contextualizing the problem and not the person. It can be helpful to point out that there are three people in the relationship right now: gambler, partner/spouse, and gambling addiction. Determine the role of gambling in the relationship from the courtship phase to the present day. Often, gambling was a positive experience or activity in the beginning, and then became more isolated and secretive as the progression continued. Some couples will benefit from completing a "timeline" together, noting all significant events since they met. It is important for the couple to include all significant events, including bereavement, loss of job(s), relocation, birth of child(ren), major wins/losses of gambling, etc. Once the timeline is complete, you can see where events cluster together and the role gambling played in their managing these events. A common one is when there is a bereavement/loss and then a gambling episode as a way of dealing with grief/loss (or more importantly avoiding the grief/loss).

When a couple is seeking therapy and the individual with a gambling disorder is focused on saving the relationship, you can use the intervention of "disarmament." This is where you get the individual to describe the "tricks of the trade" of their gambling (Ciarrocchi, 2001), and is helpful to develop a relapse prevention plan as well as identify warning signs for relapse. Learn about the people, places, and things that make it more likely they will gamble, how and when they manipulate, and ways they will lie to get money to gamble, etc. The tricks of the trade include setting passcodes/passwords on phones/computers, getting the mail before a partner gets home or converting to paperless statements sent to a different email address, referring to a friend (that doesn't exist), and using a credit card that a partner doesn't know exists. Depending on the severity of the lies and secrecy, you may consider conducting an "honesty session" where the gambler shares all the "tells" (or signs) that they have been using, and the family member is able to ask as many questions as they like during that session. When the session is over, the couple must agree to move forward and not keep rehashing the session or asking the same questions again and again.

Working with the Family: Family Only

Family members, often a partner, spouse, or parent, will seek help due to their loved one's gambling problem. A therapist may work with family and never meet the individual with a gambling disorder. Many states provide treatment funding for the family member without the requirement of the gambler present. Review confidentiality and explain how it could become a conflict of interest for you to treat the family member and then begin working with the individual with a gambling disorder at a later date. It's important to understand this because many family members are desperately seeking answers and guidance. When they receive education and guidance, they will then want their loved one to attend therapy in their place. Whenever possible, avoid this as it is viewed as a conflict of interest. Consider developing a network of certified therapists for referrals in these situations.

During initial sessions, assume the family member is coming to you in a state of crisis. Most commonly reported symptoms include trust/anger issues, depression/sadness, anxiety/fear, shock, distress, and communication problems. When people are in a state of crisis, they require a more directive approach, where you help them to sort out immediate needs and take small, actionable steps. Consider reviewing the following topics in the first few sessions, when possible.

Protect Family Members' Financial Assets

This is critical, especially if their loved one has not stopped problematic gambling. See Chapter 7: Finances for more details. In summary:

- Set up services for identity theft protection (i.e. LifeLock, Identity Guard in Canada) to make sure identity isn't being used to access additional sources of credit.
- Turn on alerts for all banking, credit card transactions, money apps, etc.
- Access credit reports on a regular basis and review for any accounts that may be open/used for gambling.
- Review bank statements or plan to visit the bank to verify if there are other accounts.
- Determine if there are any other ways to access more credit (car titles, lines of credit, payday loan accounts).

- Make a list of family and friends that need to be notified to guard against loaning any (more) money.
- Explore any other sources/access and develop a plan to reduce exposure of further financial loss.
- Encourage family members to open a separate bank account in their name only and determine how they may begin to use it for bill-paying and saving money.

Core Areas of Conflict

Often a partner/spouse is so focused on their loved one with the gambling problem that they don't give enough attention to their own physical and emotional needs. They struggle to discuss areas of conflict that are core and foundational for the relationship to recover and become even better than before the problematic gambling. Some common core areas of conflict include enabling as bailout, setting limits and boundaries, emotions and emotional regulation (e.g., trust, anger, love, confidence), and expectations of the new lifestyle, and are described below.

Enabling as a Form of Bailout

Family members don't always know that enabling actually doesn't help their loved one ultimately get better. A common definition of enable means "to help," yet with addiction it means "to help stay in active addiction." Help the partner/ spouse identify all the ways they want to help, when it actually isn't helping (e.g., getting a second job to help pay the debt caused by gambling, not talking about their feelings for fear it will cause their loved one to start gambling again).

Setting Limits and Boundaries

Setting limits and boundaries can be extremely difficult for a partner/spouse to manage as they often enjoy, or even thrive on, controlling more than their fair share of responsibilities, activities, and chores in the relationship. They need help developing a vocabulary for letting their loved one know that they will not "pick up the slack," manage more in the relationship, or accept/

settle for less. Practicing setting limits during the session is often a critical intervention as many need the therapist to role-model what is appropriate behavior and vocabulary.

Trust, Anger, Love, Confidence

As with any betrayal in a relationship, trust is often the last thing to be restored. Trust requires safety and the ability to be vulnerable in a relationship. The gambler wants to restore trust as soon as possible while the partner/spouse knows it will be the last thing to be restored. Therapists can help clients understand that expressing their feelings and not giving a time commitment is an appropriate and healthy response given all the lies and betrayal. Help the partner/spouse feel the anger at the gambling disorder while still feeling love for their partner. Oftentimes, people think they cannot have dual emotions or that they need to be clear about one feeling over another. Help them to practice *one day at a time* or even *one minute at a time* with their feelings and thoughts. As they practice this, their self-esteem and confidence will begin to improve. After recovering from the lies, betrayal, and financial devastation, many partners/spouses feel stupid, and as if they should have known. This questioning has a negative impact on their self-esteem and confidence. Help them to understand and separate their partner's actions from them.

Expectations of New Lifestyle

The partner/spouse needs to have the support of therapy to fully express and think about their new lifestyle. Some never wanted to be committed to someone who had an addiction, while others may be more excited about what the future holds as the past was much more difficult. Regardless of where the client may be about the future, help them to fully explore all aspects as there is an element of grief and loss processing that needs to occur. Accepting the future is even more difficult and sometimes even more complicated when they have not yet grieved for the past.

Remember that the early stages of therapy will be very different from the later stages. The early stages involve very practical and active steps to take to avoid gambling and future devastation. Later-stage therapy will include the intense emotions and learning to co-create the future together.

Working with the Family: Parents and the (Adult) Gambler

Working with parents and their adult children often requires a two-fold therapeutic approach. On one hand, you need to help the adult child launch into adulthood and have full responsibility and accountability for their decisions. On the other hand, you need to help the parents set limits, stop enabling (helping), and learn to let go so their children can grow.

In the early sessions, you will spend significant time focusing on finances. This is very important because it sets up for the adult child to have to adhere to the financial budget/plan and experience their own consequences if they make poor choices or re-engage in problematic gambling. At the same time, you will be working with the parents to learn to stay out of or distance themselves from doing all the work for their adult child. This is especially important when the parents want to take care of the finances (bailout) due to their own financial beliefs about debt, or when parents continue to focus their energy on their adult child instead of focusing on themselves or their marriage.

Later in the therapeutic process, you will want to help change the system rules to allow for the adult child to live independently in recovery and redefine their relationship with their parents. You may deal with resistance from the parents as they remain fearful of what might happen if their child relapses and their tendency may be to remain involved as a form of control over the addiction. Help everyone understand that the fear is real but cannot dominate the relationship dynamics.

Working with the Family: Parents and the (Adolescent) Gambler

Working with adolescents requires a thorough understanding of the adolescent brain. Until the age of 25, the brain is not fully developed and may be vulnerable to risky decision making. According to Gupta and Derevensky (2000b), comprehensive evaluation needs to include age of first gambling and if they experienced a "big win," whether they play videogames or did so when they were younger, whether they also smoke/use marijuana, drink alcohol, have a history of truancy, and gamble with a group of friends or solo. Some research studies have found the average age of first gambling experience to be around 12 (Jacobs, 2004), and sometimes as young as nine (Shaffer *et al.*, 1994; see also Wilber & Potenza, 2006). Given this, therapists will want to assess for 1) patterns of risky behaviors, even outside of a "pure" gambling environment (i.e., engagement in risky physical activity, sexual activity, lying, or stealing, etc.), 2) environmental settings (such as calendar year, like March madness, or summer breaks), 3) and planning and judgment patterns (i.e., does the adolescent make rash decisions with little planning or consideration for negative consequences?). In this way, therapists can start to understand the gambling symptomatology, knowing that it may not present similarly to adult gambling clients. Understanding the types of gambling will help determine riskier and more impulsive behavior patterns, which we would expect to see with some forms of gambling such as in-game sports betting and blackjack.

When you are working with the parents/family, you will want to identify the consequences (or lack thereof) and discipline from the parents (see also Chapter 3: Models of Intervention). If the parents are unintentionally rewarding negative behavior, you want to help them develop consequences that have meaning and impact, and can be delivered close in time to the targeted behavior.

The initial sessions should identify the severity of gambling behavior and financial impact. Also discuss possible co-occurring mental health disorders that could be exasperating gambling behavior (e.g., ADHD, bipolar) and whether a psychiatric evaluation should be considered. Discuss suicidality and help parents understand what they can do when they are concerned for their child's safety. Determine if their child needs a higher level of care or inpatient care for co-occurring disorders. If they can remain at home, help the parents to understand ways to redirect their child away from boredom and idle time, to keeping busy with homework, projects, chores around the house, possible part-time employment, etc. Also direct parents to implementing financial safety plans (see also Chapter 7: Finances) and creating more accountability and transparency with their child's access to money and possessions.

Adolescents gamble for a variety of reasons. Determining the root causes of gambling will help develop effective interventions for parents. Educate parents that gambling can be 1) a chance to win money, 2) exciting, 3) a way to spend time with friends, 4) a distraction from everyday life, 5) a way to fit in or be accepted, 6) a means of feeling important, and 7) perceived as an easy way to get rich quick. Adolescent gamblers also report having lower self-esteem compared to their peers, are prone to engage in multiple co-occurring addictive behaviors (smoking, drinking, drug use/abuse), and have a greater need for sensation seeking. Adolescents will dissociate more frequently while gambling, which helps to explain the risk-taking and impulsivity and the inability to stop. They also have more difficulty conforming to social norms and experience more issues with self-discipline.

Effective parenting, remaining consistent, and not allowing things to fall back into old patterns is critical for the success of adolescents stopping excessive gambling and beginning to launch successfully into young adulthood.

Working with the Family: Final Stage of Therapy

Regardless of family, couples, or parent/child work, the final stage of therapy focuses on discharge planning. Did each family member meet their treatment goals? What is their view of whether the individual with a gambling disorder has met their treatment goals? Is there a need for additional treatment? How can you keep the door open for the family to re-engage at a later date?

Develop *Warning Signs for Relapse* that are co-created as a family. For instance, if the passcode on the phone returns, the gambler is more irritable on the weekends during sports season, does not wanting to attend meetings, or stops listening to recovery-related podcasts, these are all warning signs that the person is at risk for relapse. Discuss how the family should provide feedback and communicate their concerns with warning signs. Take the exercise one step further and have each family member identify their own warning signs and triggers to relapsing into old behaviors. Remember that it is an entire system that will feel the effects when one person is triggered or in relapse mode.

Conclusion

Taken together, while a gambler's family will no doubt be unique and idio-syncratic in terms of the membership and makeup of family members, it is clear that all members of the gambler's family are impacted and influenced by the gambling disorder. Harm to the gambler's family may vary in terms of financial stress and adversity, loss of assets and property, intrapersonal conflicts particularly around trust and distrust, and similar socio-cultural aspects of the family dynamic. However, by taking a new perspective (from First Order Change to Second Order Change), therapists can help families create new and adaptive familial systems, in hopes of getting to a new homeo-stasis (equilibrium) as a family unit.

CHAPTER 9 SELF-HELP AND PEER SUPPORTS

"There is a kind of understanding that only someone who has already been there, gets."

It is widely accepted that each person has their own unique road to recovery. Each of us may know people who benefited from psychotherapy alone, or in combination with 12-Step programs, and still others who have been successful at "stopping cold turkey" without any help from therapists or self-help groups. Regardless of anecdotal stories, it is the duty of therapists to make sure clients are fully informed of all the options available to them, and treatments that have been shown to be effective for people, rather than myths or folklore treatments.

It is important that therapists refrain from giving clients an "addiction" diagnosis, such that they believe the client must agree to complete abstinence at the beginning of seeking help. We can't approach all clients seeking help for gambling problems as if they already have an addiction and require total lifelong abstinence. As such, the current chapter will focus on several self-help options for clients with gambling disorder. While self-help programs have been shown to be helpful and effective for clients, it is important to remember that each client served is different, and a one-size-fits-all approach to treatment will not be (and is not) effective.

Self-Help Programs

Self-help programs have existed around the world for many decades. Whether shame, guilt, stigma, or financial barriers keep individuals from asking for help, some will choose self-help before professional help. Others will learn about self-help from professionals, and still others will access many forms of self-help after completing professional counseling.

The definition of self-help is the act of bettering oneself or overcoming one's problems without the help or aid or assistance of another. Self-help programs are known as mutual help, mutual aid, or support groups, and consist of a group of people who provide mutual support to each other. Self-help groups imply any group of people who share a common issue, and there is not a professional leading the group. They are self-governing and do not have group affiliations or receive outside support or funding.

12-Step Programs

12-Step Programs are self-help programs focusing on the issues of addiction and recovery. They have a set of guiding principles (12 steps) outlining a course of action for recovery. Many therapists are familiar with 12-Step groups that include Alcoholics Anonymous (AA), Narcotics Anonymous (NA), and Gamblers Anonymous (GA). These 12-Step programs also offer self-help for family members such as Al-anon, Nar-anon, and Gam-anon.

Gamblers Anonymous

The Fellowship of Gamblers Anonymous (GA; Gamblers Anonymous, 2000) began in 1957 with their first meeting held in Los Angeles, California. Meetings continued to expand geographically, and it is reported that GA exists worldwide in the United States, Canada, Australia, New Zealand, Great Britain, Uganda, Israel, and many other countries. The requirement remains the same today: *the desire to stop gambling*. Anyone that attends GA meetings can find help, support, and some advice regarding legal difficulties, employment issues, family problems, and financial difficulties.

There are several types of GA meetings and it is important to educate your clients about the differences. *Regular Therapy Meetings* are for the individual with a gambling problem. GA literature is read at the beginning of the meeting, all or parts of the "Combo" book is read, and members are reminded to respect anonymity (what is said in here, stays in here). *Closed Meetings* are meetings that are reserved for only those identifying as having a gambling problem. *Open Meetings* are open to those who may not identify with having a gambling problem. The Open Meetings are a great place for paraprofessionals and professionals to attend to learn and experience firsthand what a GA meeting is all about. *Discussion Step Meetings* are more focused on discussing the 12 Steps of recovery and how you interpret a particular step. Many Step Meetings will use the entire meeting to focus on a deeper discussion of one step. *Combined GA and Gam-anon Meetings* allow everyone to come together to strengthen the understanding between the fellowships. Many forms of combined meetings can exist, including two chairpersons, two guest speakers, half of a GA meeting and then half of a Gam-anon meeting, and so on. Websites and printed meeting lists will include all of these types of meeting details (i.e., Closed, Open, Step).

In addition to the meetings themselves, it is helpful to familiarize yourself with other aspects of GA to better educate and inform your clients on how to benefit fully from the fellowship. *Intergroup* is a subset of GA members in a geographical area that serves to discuss mutual issues, keep the lines of communication open between groups, and serve in more public settings. Often the members have more clean time and can be of service to other members and groups. *Pressure Relief Meeting* is unique to GA and is a vital and necessary tool for many members. The purpose is to relieve pressure, mostly financial, but also personal, employment, and legal pressure. As a therapist, you need to know when a client may benefit from such a meeting with other GA members. Often, the financial pressures can be complex and seem impossible to solve. Pressure Relief Meetings can help prioritize, develop, or modify a restitution plan, and help the member stay focused on "one day at a time" with their recovery program. Combining Pressure Relief Meetings with therapy and financial restitution treatment goals can be extremely effective for your clients and their families.

Pinning Ceremony and pins (or symbols) are given to members when they achieve specific abstinence and/or attendance milestones. Not all GA groups do this, so it is important to know more about your region's practices. There may be times when a client or former client invites you to their pinning ceremony. You will need to determine if you are allowed to attend, based on your organization's policies. If you are able to attend, you also need to consider whether you will see other clients or former clients, and if this is a conflict of interest. You must be able to preserve client confidentiality at all times. Make sure to fully discuss any attendance requests with peers, supervisors, and other clinical colleagues who can help determine if it will help or hurt to attend.

Celebrate Recovery

Celebrate Recovery is a Christ-centered 12-step program for anyone struggling with hurt, pain, or an addiction of any kind (Celebrate Recovery, 2018). Many of these programs exist within churches but have also expanded to recovery houses, rescue missions, universities, and prisons around the world. Celebrate Recovery (CR) is similar to Gamblers Anonymous, with a religious biblical emphasis. Many clients that either want to return to their faith or want faith to be a part of their recovery may benefit from CR programs and their format. CR has 12 steps and eight principles that are very similar to 12-Step but add the biblical comparisons.

When considering this type of self-help for your clients, make sure you know where the nearest CR programs are located. Visit the website, make calls, and become fully informed about the CR programs in your area. Depending on the program, there may not be a group specifically for gambling addiction but a more general addiction group. Help your clients to understand how to actively participate and even educate others about the similarities and differences in gambling addiction as compared to substance addictions and sex addictions. CR also has Codependency Groups which may be a good fit when working with partners/spouses/parents. These may be available in geographical areas where Gam-anon is not available.

SMART Recovery

Self-Management And Recovery Training (SMART) is a global community of mutual-support groups (Smart Recovery, 2020). SMART Recovery groups are rooted in a science-based and 4-Point Program®. SMART Recovery has both in-person and online meetings. This program addresses addiction and ways to resolve problems associated with addiction. There is no guarantee that an in-person meeting will be solely dedicated to a specific addiction (e.g., gambling), but it will address how to resolve problems regardless of the type of addiction. Similar to Celebrate Recovery, therapists will need to verify if and where the in-person meetings are located in your geographical area.

Online Meetings

SMART Recovery was one of the first to offer online meetings. This may be a useful tool for clients, especially if transportation is an issue, or they live in a rural setting with fewer resources available. In addition to the online meetings, the SMART website also provides specialized groups and peer support forums.

Peer Supports

According to SAMHSA, peer supports encompass a range of activities and interactions between people who share similar experiences of being diagnosed with mental health conditions, substance-use disorders, or gambling disorders (Peers, n.d.). Peer supports offer a level of acceptance, understanding, and validation not found in many other professional relationships (Bringing Recovery Supports to Scale, 2017). And by sharing their own lived experience and practical guidance, peer support workers help people to develop their own goals, create strategies for self-empowerment, and take concrete steps towards building fulfilling, self-determined lives for themselves. A peer support worker, often referred to as a peer support specialist, is someone who has lived experience of recovery from mental health, substance-use, or gambling disorders. They provide non-clinical, strength-based support and are "experientially credentialed" by their own recovery journey. Peer support specialists are well known in the substance-use treatment field. They are relatively new to the field of gambling treatment. You may find a peer support specialist teamed up with a therapist for inpatient, group, or family sessions. The role of the peer support specialist complements and does not duplicate or replace the role of a therapist, case manager, or other members of a treatment team. They bring their own personal knowledge of what it is like to live and thrive with a mental health, substance-use, or gambling disorder. Emerging research (Substance Abuse and Mental Health Services Administration, 2020) shows peer support specialists are effective in supporting recovery. This includes increased self-esteem and confidence, increased sense of control and ability to bring about change in their lives, increased sense that treatment is responsive and inclusive of needs, increased empathy and acceptance, increased engagement, self-care, and wellness, and an increase in social supports and social functioning.

As a therapist working with gambling disorders, it's important to identify if there are any peer support specialists in your area. Getting to know and work with peer support specialists can make all the difference in the recovery of your clients. Ideally, you will want the option to give their name and number to some of your clients, maybe to meet them for coffee, to go to their first GA or other self-help meeting, or anything related to recovery. A peer support specialist can also refer people to you for professional help. It is a two-way relationship with the primary goal of helping people with gambling disorders get the help they need and deserve.

Many people in recovery for gambling disorder may choose to become a peer support specialist as part of their ongoing recovery program. You can help your clients have hope for a better future, and even future career opportunities.

Having the Conversation

Now that you know more about self-help programs, have a conversation with your client about the usefulness of these meetings. Counseling is not supposed to be forever, and getting your client involved in a fellowship that can be lifelong is a great tool. Take Gamblers Anonymous (GA), for example. It is recommended that you attend a GA meeting in your area to learn more about the people and the locations, and to establish a working partnership with GA. Ideally, you should meet some members that are part of the local Intergroup and ask for their permission to give their name and phone number to clients who may be new to the idea of 12-Step. GA needs therapists and therapists need GA.

Consider asking your client to attend at least four meetings, including the initial meeting, before determining if it is right for them long-term. When we give "homework" that is time-limited, often our clients can commit because it doesn't feel like a forever commitment. Also give your client the opportunity to share what they liked and disliked about a meeting, as a way of helping them to become fully informed and empowered. Create a worksheet and ask your client to complete it at the end of a self-help meeting. The worksheet can include information such as: type of self-help meeting, location, duration, number of people in attendance, general topics that were discussed, how they treat "newcomers," three things they liked about the meeting, three things they didn't like, and other impressions/comments. By having this as homework, it helps the person maintain some distance and hopefully remain more open to the experience.

Understanding the Younger Generations

It's important to understand all the generational characteristics of the individuals that you treat. For many years, Baby Boomers and Generation X have made up the majority of therapists' client caseloads. Today, however, therapists are now seeing a shift to include Millennials and even Generation Z as adults in therapy. Anyone born between the years 1981 and 1996 (Pew Research Center, 2019) is considered a Millennial and anyone born from 1997 onward is part of Generation Z.

So, what does self-help have to do with generational characteristics? We know that Millennials are digital natives. They have always had technology growing up and the way that they seek information and even seek help is very different from Baby Boomers and Generation X. Millennials will use apps, Google everything first, and review websites before ever picking up the phone and making a call. They would prefer a digital solution for most everything, including self-help. Unless a 12-Step meeting is well known for having younger members, most Millennials will not commit long-term to 12-Step or GA specifically. As a therapist, you will need to have other options and answers for these younger generations. Many of these answers exist online.

Other Online Supports

In an age where everything lives on the Internet, our clients can find recovery and other peer supports online. At the time of this publication, Facebook private groups, homegrown Skype support meetings, podcasts, and various apps provide "communities" for sharing and collaborating with each other (around the world). Become familiar with what is available and discuss this with your clients during sessions. Help your clients to practice safe behavior on the Internet by discussing how to protect their anonymity, what to share and what not to share online, and how to get the most out of these discussions, chats, and support forums.

This chapter introduces you to more than just 12-Step as a self-help tool for your clients. Effective therapy for gambling addiction should include an introduction to self-help support groups for your clients. You need to become familiar with all the options in your geographical region and develop relationships that can assist your clients. Becoming not only familiar with but confident in the various technological options for support will be imperative in your work with Millennials and Gen Z clients.

CHAPTER 10
THE LEGAL SYSTEM AND GAMBLING

"Act as if you are already in front of the judge."

As a therapist, there are many pathways of involvement with the legal system. One common pathway is to work with clients who also have some legal oversight, such as probation/parole, or who have been court-ordered to complete treatment. A second pathway is to work directly in the criminal justice system in some clinical capacity such as jails, alternative sentencing sites, and step-down units. A third pathway involves a therapist working with a client's attorney due to open or pending charges against the client. This third pathway is often where a therapist is least prepared and confident about what to do, how to do things, and what to communicate, when. The idea of getting a subpoena to share documentation, being court-ordered to testify, or providing expert testimony are professional skills that many therapists are under-prepared to handle or rarely have opportunities to become skilled and competent in.

When problem gambling and gambling disorders are added to legal issues, many of us are even less confident about what to do and how to navigate the legal system with our clients. It is critical to keep in mind that gambling disorders may not be protected under public policies, depending upon country and jurisdiction. In the United States, for instance, gambling disorders are not protected under the Americans with Disabilities Act (ADA, 1990), although alcohol and substance-use disorders are. While this mostly applies to protection from employment discrimination, there is still no federal oversight for gambling disorder, and it is important to proceed with caution about what is shared, with whom, and for what purpose(s), in order to protect our clients.

At the same time, take advantage of any opportunities to educate the legal system about gambling disorders, especially the judge who is deciding sentencing. According to the National Institute of Justice's *Research for Practice* (2004), several key findings answered questions about why people commit crime due to their gambling problem, and to what extent gambling occurs in the prison system. The percentage of problem and disordered gamblers among arrestees was three to five times higher than the general population, and nearly one-third of arrestees identified as compulsive gamblers admitted to committing robbery in the previous year (National Institute of Justice, 2004). Additionally, research indicates that roughly 50% of all problem gamblers participate in criminal activity (National Institute of Justice, 2004). The majority of crimes committed by problem gamblers are for the purposes of getting money to gamble or to pay off gambling debts. Lastly, one in five compulsive gamblers who had been arrested admitted to having sold drugs to finance their gambling (National Institute of Justice, 2004).

Gambler or Criminal Profile

Before diving into what to do, when, and how, let's step back and take time to determine which profile best fits our client. The concept of these profiles was originally developed by the first author, Jody Bechtold, and evolved from working in substance disorder treatment centers in the United States, where 100% of the clients were probation- or parole-mandated to attend a Night Intensive Outpatient Program (NIOP). After a few years, it became easy to quickly assess which clients were 1) drug addicts who committed crime, or 2) criminals who used drugs.

The first profile, "addict," struggles greatly to remain abstinent from drugs and/or alcohol and generally has a good rapport with probation/parole officers and staff. They are not focused on "getting over" as much as getting help for their addiction. They struggle to get and maintain clean time, and their involvement with the legal system occurred long after they developed an addiction. The second profile, "criminal," is able to abstain from drugs rather effortlessly, especially if they were incarcerated for a period of time before entering addiction treatment. However, they struggle to follow the rules, even the small ones, on a consistent basis. They were involved in the legal system, often as juveniles and before developing an addiction to drugs. Clients were asked: "If you knew it was a school holiday, yet the school zone flashing lights were blinking, would you slow down since it is the law or would you disregard the reduced speed limit?" As you can imagine, the "criminal" doesn't take any time to think and simply states that it is a holiday so the law doesn't apply. The "addict," however, pauses to think through the consequences of obeying the flashing light vs. ignoring it due to the holiday.

Understanding these profiles with respect to gambling may help you determine the approach to take with treatment goals, type and frequency of communication with the legal system, and what would be alternative sentencing options. The "gambler" who commits crime will most likely do well in GA meetings and the GA fellowship, respond favorably to interventions that "close the doors" to gambling, and will reconnect with family and friends. They will struggle with abstinence and often have multiple relapses before they have significant clean time. They will commit to therapy, appreciate the therapeutic alliance, and agree to most recommendations. The "criminal" who gambles will find ways to break the rules, even those not related to gambling. They will spend more effort controlling, lying, and keeping the chaos as a distraction from their criminal activities. They will easily wear a "mask," presenting as if they are working hard at recovery, while their criminal activity or gambling is ongoing.

Another way to understand these two profiles is to think of two of the Cluster B personality disorders in the DSM-5: antisocial and narcissistic. Antisocial personality disorder has features of lying, disregard for right vs. wrong, and using wit or charm to manipulate others. The "criminal" who gambles often disregards right from wrong in several areas of their life, not just related to gambling. Narcissistic personality disorder includes features of a grandiose sense of self, preoccupied with fantasies of success, belief that he/she is special and unique, and a sense of entitlement. The "addict" who commits crime initially was driven by ego and belief that they had a gift for gambling and winning. They eventually break the law directly related to their gambling activities, most often non-violent, white-collar crimes (i.e. identity theft, passing bad checks). The change to gambling disorder in the DSM-5, which removed the "commits illegal acts such as forgery, fraud, theft, or embezzlement to finance gambling" criterion, unfortunately makes it more difficult to educate the legal system. However, this removal was made because it was not a criterion that would exclude someone from meeting the minimum criteria. It was often the last criterion to be met, long after enough other criteria had been met for a diagnosis of gambling disorder (American Psychiatric Association, 2013). In other words, if someone said "no" to this criterion, it didn't impact the overall score of needing five or more to meet the criteria for a gambling disorder.

Legal Involvement: Before and During

Therapists need to provide effective clinical care with clients regardless of their involvement in the legal system. However, for some therapists, it is unclear how the legal system will view a client's actions? Will the legal system see these actions as operating from "free will," or will the system see gambling disorders as a disease and the person's actions as being a result of their illness? Furthermore, the courts need to consider the victims and seriousness of the crime(s) committed. While these questions are important, they are not necessarily for the therapist to focus on. Instead, we recommend that therapists approach all clients with a gambling disorder as if they will have some interaction with the legal system and at some point this may involve the therapist.

When working with gambling clients in the legal system, it is imperative that therapists discuss limitations (including potential subpoena of records) in informed consents, utilize evidence-based screens and assessments in initial intake, and include discussion about the therapeutic role and clinical documentation should you be court-ordered to share or provide clinical testimony. Clients need to know where the boundaries are, even in therapy sessions. It is critical for therapists to follow the evidence-based screens and assessments for gambling disorders, particularly if they have to report on the outcomes later (see Chapter 5: Where to Start and What to Ask). Practice good clinical documentation skills with respect to progress notes and psychotherapy notes. Include the hypothesis, internal dialogue regarding your client, and impressions about your client in the *psychotherapy note* section (which, in the United States, is protected by the Privacy Rule of Health Insurance Portability and Accountability Act (HIPAA) (2004)). *Progress notes* should include all things that are measurable or the client verbally "reports." Examples include date and time of the session (including duration); whether the client reported gambling or remaining abstinent; whether they reported attending GA or other self-help meetings; homework follow-up and outcome; self-exclusion or other programs as status updates; financial budget and restitution adherence; employment status; medication adherence; family involvement; and any other measurable activities.

The 5 Rs of Treatment and Documentation

The 5 Rs (i.e., Remorse, Repentance, Restitution, Rehabilitation, and Recovery) will help therapists to evaluate the client and have a framework for providing clinical impressions. Share these five terms with clients and discuss specific examples of what they are doing or can start doing. This can help them to focus their time and energy while in treatment. Best practices include making sure you can answer "What makes you say that?" after every statement. You want to be consistent in reporting factual information that you can measure. If you have difficulty answering "What makes you say that?" then you need to revisit your statement and determine what is factual and how you know. For example, if you state that your client is committed to a recovery lifestyle, you need to give evidence of this statement with measurable behaviors—behaviors such as working two jobs, attending 12-Step meetings, spending time with others in recovery, and adhering to a financial restitution plan. Now, the challenge is to give measurable evidence of each of those behaviors. How do you measure working two jobs, attending 12-Step, spending time with others in recovery, and following a financial plan? Release of information (ROI) signed with both bosses to verify work attendance, slips signed at 12-Step, ROI and session attendance with key people in the client's life, and audit review of bank statements showing payments by check to people for specified amounts.

Let's look at the 5 Rs closely.

- *Remorse*—deep regret or guilt for a wrong committed. In what ways has the client expressed and/or shown remorse? Have they verbalized that they were sorry for what they did? What makes you say that?
- *Repentance*—admitting wrong and changing behavior in the future. Have they acknowledged that what they did was wrong? Are they engaging in behaviors that demonstrate change? What makes you say that?
- *Restitution*—restoring something lost or stolen to its proper owner. Are they willing to pay back the money that was stolen? Do they acknowledge that there are no victimless crimes? What makes you say that?
- *Rehabilitation*—the action of restoring someone to health or normal life by training and therapy after imprisonment, addiction, or illness. Make sure to comment whether a person can return to a healthy lifestyle (rehab) or if they need to learn for the first time (habilitation) how to live a recovery lifestyle. Do they have multiple incarcerations or inpatient rehabs, and they still are unable to live a recovery lifestyle?
- *Recovery*—a return to a normal state of health, mind, or strength. Does the person accept recovery as a process or are they only willing to abstain from certain behaviors? Are they attending a 12-Step program and involved and invested in it, or are they merely attending to get their attendance slip signed?

Overall, keep answering "What makes you say that?" and have answers that "are evidenced by…" This will keep you from only reporting opinions and help you focus on more objective data and behaviors. See the sample report at the end of the chapter.

Act as if You Are Already in Front of the Judge

As therapists, we never know when we might learn of criminal behavior from a client. We can't go back in time and do things differently, so always "act as if you're in front of the judge" from the start with clinical sessions, documentation, communication, and interactions. If a client comes to you after several months of working together to share they have been recently arrested and have secured an attorney, what would you do differently moving forward in the therapeutic relationship? Learn more about why they were arrested and begin to focus on the 5 Rs. Determine which Releases of Information will be necessary in communicating with their attorney and other legal staff. Make a point to talk with their legal team as early as possible to better understand what they will need from you. An example may include providing all your documentation to their forensic expert or providing testimony at the trial (two extremes). If you or your agency have policies regarding your involvement in the legal system, do you consider referring to another gambling addiction therapist? All of these issues need to be explored as soon as you learn more about your client. This is when we move to the "during" phase, and need to position how we will continue to work with our client while they navigate through the legal system.

Two different scenarios emerge at this point: 1) the client does not confess or plead guilty; or 2) the client pleads guilty. If you find yourself in the first scenario, you will want to fully understand what your client's attorney will be expecting from you. Some may be looking for a written report or providing testimony in court, but you want to fully understand your role with respect to the gambling disorder/behavior and the charges. Do not go outside your scope of competence, and seek supervision/peer consultation as necessary. The second scenario is much more common for clinical providers to find themselves in. You are not required to provide any information or evidence to help or not help your client, as they have already pleaded guilty. Your role is to provide clinical information useful to the attorney and judge for sentencing determination or alternative sentencing recommendations.

Sometimes, writing a full report, even if just for practice, can help make you stay true to facts and evidence, and rely less on subjective feelings and opinions. It may also help you and your client determine treatment goals while waiting for the sentencing hearing.

Clinical Report Sections

Here are suggested sections and types of information you will want to include in your clinical report.

A *Qualifications of the evaluator/therapist:* give all your qualifying information including your license, your gambling certification level and what it means to get this certification (hours, exam), and whether you have conducted research and/or presented at local, state, and national conferences on this topic.

B *Reason for the evaluation and assessment of the client:* who referred your client to you, for what reason(s).

Definition of gambling and prevalence rates: define gambling, identify all the forms of gambling, and cite research of estimated lifetime gambling rates.

Gambling problems in the general and criminal populations: include statistics of arrestees and inmates as these relate to problematic gambling, alternative sentencing options at local or state level, and prevalence of gambling activities that occur while incarcerated.

South Oaks Gambling Screen (SOGS; Lesieur & Blume, 1987).

Problem Gambling Severity Index (PGSI; Ferris & Wyane, 2006): give background, authors, scoring, and reliability/validity statistics.

Define Gambling Disorder, DSM-5/ICD-11, and list each criterion with cutoff scores.

Biopsychosocial formulations: include aspects related to biopsychosocial factors that result from gambling disorder (see also Chapter 2: Understanding Gambling Disorder). Also consider research regarding bio-neurological factors (including norepinephrine and dopaminergic systems), psychological factors (including cognitive distortions, habituation, chasing, etc.), and sociocultural factors (including history of abuse/neglect/trauma, parents who gamble or use drugs/alcohol, etc.).

Psychiatric co-occurrences: provide research to support the frequent co-occurrence of psychiatric disorders with gambling disorders. Include suicidality and research about elevated rates with gambling disorders.

Adverse effects of atypical antipsychotic medications: include the latest research regarding medications that can cause excessive gambling. This section is especially important if the client has a history of medications prescribed for impulse-control problems.

C   *Client background:* past social and developmental history, family interviews and/or involvement, medical history, past psychiatric history, gambling problems beginning with when client first began to gamble, comment on action/escape and pathways model, give examples of compulsion to gamble, and link to all addictive disorders that eventually make a person continue despite consequences. Comment on other addictive behaviors and the intersection of them with gambling. Also comment on any other traumatic episodes and where they fall on a timeline.

Previous treatment: discuss any and all previous treatment and any outcomes. This is also important if the client has never had treatment before.

Family interview: conduct interviews with family to better understand the timeline of gambling and criminal behavior.

Clinical evaluation: utilize evidence-based tools such as the South Oaks Gambling Screen (SOGS; Lesieur & Blume, 1987), Problem Gambling Severity Index (PGSI; Ferris and Wyane, 2006); see also Chapter 5: Where to Start and What to Ask, and give background, authors, scoring, and reliability/validity statistics.

Diagnosis: provide all formal diagnosis per the DSM-5 or ICD-11 and include relevant information to support. It is recommended to spell out the criteria for gambling disorder and whether the client meets and evidence to support.

Consider the use of Becks Depression Inventory (BDI; Beck *et al.*, 1961) or other scales such as the Patient Health Questionnaire-9 (PHQ-9; Kroenke, Spitzer, & Wiliams, 2001) to support additional diagnosis.

Ask questions about the client's overall timeline and examples of behaviors that provide a comprehensive story.

Recommendations for treatment: include types of therapy modalities and response to or reason for recommending. If the client has been in therapy for a while, consider giving treatment outcomes that comment on the following: treatment attendance, medication management, financial budget, financial restitution plan and compliance, financial protection plan, self-exclusion, 12-Step (GA) attendance and involvement, family involvement, employment, and any other noteworthy information that supports your recommendations and conclusions.

Recovery: clinical impression of whether the client's ability and willingness for recovery exists; include 12-Step (GA) attendance, financial restitution plan, financial budget, self-exclusion activities, family involvement and supports, medication adherence, recovery from other addictions, and prior attempts at recovery before legal involvement.

Other recommendations: consider this section for requesting treatment during incarceration or alternative sentencing based on the past issues. This is your opportunity to educate the judge and court. Include treatment levels of care, intensity, and network of services. Caution against mandating specific number of 12-Step meetings per week since it is unlikely that daily GA meetings exist in a given area. The concepts of getting a sponsor and 90-in-90 are not as applicable with GA as with AA or NA. Also caution again mandating self-exclusion as it isn't voluntary if the court orders it.

Legal Involvement: After

Many therapists have worked with clients that were on probation or parole. When working with clients on probation or parole, it is recommended to meet with or communicate with the probation/parole officer and determine how involved they will be with the client. You may have experienced everything from extremely intensive to monthly check-ins and everything in between. Most probation and parole officers have a good working knowledge of drug and alcohol addiction/recovery but do not know much about gambling disorders. Use any and every opportunity to educate them about how to measure relapses, what would be considered too many relapses, the importance of the financial restitution budget and plan as part of recovery, and other types of gambling behaviors that may go undetected (lottery tickets, fantasy sports betting, online gambling, etc.). Provide concrete and factual reporting that includes therapy attendance, financial management progress, family involvement, 12-Step or other self-help attendance, and the importance of employment as recovery.

It's recommended that you keep your client in therapy for an extended period of time (calendar days) while also stepping them down to less frequent sessions. For example, client X has been in therapy for over two years but has only been seen monthly for the past six months. Having a client remain accountable and responsible is a key component of recovery. While clients want to be "free," they also are scared to be on their own. Help them slowly to manage their daily life while still attending therapy, even if it is only once a month.

Providing Expert Testimony

For many therapists, the idea of providing testimony in court is anxiety-provoking and something many may choose to avoid. However, most of the anxiety and fear evoked by the idea of providing testimony is a result of a lack of education or knowledge about what is needed as part of the expert testimony process.

So, what is expert testimony? *Expert testimony* is the *testimony* made by a qualified person about a scientific, technical, or professional issue. An *expert* is often called upon to *testify* due to their familiarity with the subject or special training in the field. Based on this definition, you can understand why you may be called upon to provide your expertise as a certified gambling addiction counselor. This is often an opportunity to advocate, educate, and impact the legal system with respect to gambling disorders. Depending on the court (state or federal), you may or may not qualify as an expert to testify. The legal system will determine if you meet the requirements based on your education and certification, and whether you have provided other evaluations prior to testifying. Many of us will provide written evaluations that are submitted to the court and that will be the extent of it. Take any opportunity to educate and advocate about gambling disorders.

Understanding the legal system and your potential involvement as a therapist is very important. Act as if you are already in front of the judge by reviewing your informed consents, releases of information, and privacy policies to be fully prepared if and when you need to provide expert testimony or share clinical evaluations and impressions. Always seek peer supervision and consultation before submitting a report to an attorney or judge.

The following report is an example for expert testimony. Typically, you would write such a report after interviewing the client, family, and other important individuals that can contribute to the overall picture of the gambling behavior. While this report is not the format for reporting your own client treatment outcomes, it does provide an overview of the content needed to consider when providing expert testimony.

Example Report Evaluation to Inform and Educate Sentencing

A   *Qualifications of the evaluator/therapist*: Jody Bechtold is a Licensed Clinical Social Worker (LCSW) in the state of Pennsylvania. She also holds Internationally Certified Gambling Counselor Level II (ICGC) and Board Approved Clinical Consultant (BACC) certifications with the International Gambling Counselor Certification Board. To obtain these certifications, the evaluator/therapist has accumulated over 2000 hours of direct clinical work with gamblers and family/support members. She is the CEO of The Better Institute where 40% of her clinical caseload is with individuals with gambling disorders and family members. In addition to clinical experience, the evaluator has provided expert testimony for federal cases in Allegheny County since 2011. In addition to clinical experience, the evaluator has delivered presentations specific to gambling addiction at local, state, national, and international conferences since 2007.

B   *Reason for the evaluation and assessment of the client*: Bob Smith is a 65-year-old, widowed, Caucasian male currently residing with his brother. His Federal Public Defender, Mr. AD, requested a gambling disorder specific evaluation for the defendant.

Definition of gambling and prevalence rates: Gambling is defined as risking something you have, in hopes of gaining something you don't have, when the outcome is uncertain. Many forms of legal and illegal gambling exist in the United States and include lotteries, bingo, card gambling, sports betting, electronic gambling machines (including slot machines), social casino gambling, and other online games of chance. Multiple research studies have found 76%–86% of US adults gamble at least once in their lives.

Gambling problems in the general and criminal populations: It is estimated that between 1% and 5% of the US adult population meets the criteria for a gambling disorder in a given year. But is there a connection between problem gambling and crime? Do compulsive gamblers resort to criminal activity to pay their debts and finance their bets? In the *National Institute of Justice Research for Practice Journal* of 2004: "Gambling and Crime among Arrestees: Exploring the Link," several key findings answered these questions. The percentage of problem and disordered gamblers among arrestees was three to five times higher than the general population. And nearly one-third of arrestees identified as compulsive gamblers admitted to committing robbery in the previous year. Additionally, the research indicates that roughly 50% of all problem gamblers participate in criminal activity. The majority of crimes committed by problem gamblers are for the purposes of getting money to gamble or pay off gambling debts. Male compulsive gamblers typically began gambling as teenagers. Lastly, one in five compulsive gamblers who had been arrested admitted to having sold drugs to finance their gambling.

South Oaks Gambling Screen (Lesieur & Blume, 1987) is a self-report gambling screen originally based on DSM-III criteria for pathological gambling. It is widely used in clinical and epidemiological studies and has high internal consistency (Cronbach's alpha = 0.97 and 0.86, respectively; Lesieur & Blume, 1987; Stinchfield, 2002) and adequate test–retest reliability (r = 0.71; Lesieur & Blume, 1987) with clinical populations. Scores range from 0 to 20; a score of 3 or 4 indicates possible problem gambling, and a score of 5 or more is indicative of pathological gambling (Lesieur & Blume, 1987).

Problem Gambling Severity Index (2001) is a widely used nine-item scale for measuring the severity of gambling problems in the general population. Scores range from 0 to 27, categorizing risk into four categories: Non-Problem, Low Risk, Moderate Risk, and Severe Risk for a gambling problem.

Gambling Disorder (F63.0): The 5th edition of the *Diagnostic and Statistical Manual* (DSM-5) of the American Psychiatric Association (APA, 2013) defines gambling disorder as meeting four or more of the nine criteria in the past 12 months.

1   Need to gamble with increasing amount of money to achieve the desired excitement

2   Restless or irritable when trying to cut down or stop gambling

3   Repeated unsuccessful efforts to control, cut back on, or stop gambling

4   Frequent thoughts about gambling (such as reliving past gambling

experiences, planning the next gambling venture, thinking of ways to get money to gamble)

5   Often gambling when feeling distressed

6   After losing money gambling, often returning to get even (referred to as "chasing" one's losses)

7   Lying to conceal gambling activity

8   Jeopardizing or losing a significant relationship, job, or educational/career opportunity because of gambling

9   Relying on others to help with money problems caused by gambling

The disorder was reclassified in the category of "Substance-related and Addictive Disorders" with the change based on similarities between substance-use and gambling disorders.

Biopsychosocial formulations: Much research has been performed recently in the area of disordered gambling (Institute for Research on Pathological Gambling and Related Disorders, 2006; Potenza, 2006). The field of psychiatry has also had substantial increase in neurobiological studies investigating pathological gambling. The research primarily investigates the neurotransmitters of serotonin, dopamine, norepinephrine, and opioids. The research hypothesizes that these systems are particularly important for various aspects of disordered gambling; serotonin underlying impulse-control, dopamine differential reward and reinforcement, norepinephrine arousal and excitement, and opioids pleasure and urges (Potenza, 2008). Additional research continues to investigate the noradrenergic systems and the role of glutamates. All of these have implications for pharmacological interventions.

Psychiatric co-occurrences: Co-occurrences with psychiatric disorders and disordered gambling have been observed in both clinical and community-based research. However, the nature of the co-occurrences between problem and disordered gambling and psychiatric disorders remains incompletely understood. For instance, self-control and impulsivity have been found to be associated with disordered gambling (Blanco *et al.*, 2009). Similarly, problem and disordered gambling is more prevalent in individuals with schizophrenia than in the general population with frequencies ranging from 5% to 20% in clinical samples (Desai & Potenza, 2009). Schizophrenia is also associated with elevated rates of substance-use disorders (SUDs), which are frequently comorbid with problem/disordered gambling in the general population and may develop via shared mechanisms. The frequent co-occurrence between problem/disordered gambling and SUDs suggests shared mechanisms in schizophrenia. And this relationship may help explain the impairment in self-control and decision making for individuals with all three disorders.

Adverse effects of atypical antipsychotic medications: Impulse-control problems are thought to be influenced by temperamental, genetic, and physiological risk factors. Dopamine receptor agonists have been implicated in some cases. In May of 2016, the FDA released a safety warning regarding the association of aripiprazole (Abilify) with increased urges for gambling, binge-eating, hypersexuality, and increased spending. Dopamine receptor agonists have been implicated in some cases as they may cause impulse-control problems by producing a hyperdopaminergic state in the mesolimbic pathway (reward system). Aripiprazole is a unique second-generation antipsychotic with partial agonist properties at the dopamine D2 receptor and D3 receptor regions of the brain. In June of 2016, the FDA released a safety warning regarding dopamine agonists, Requip and Mirapex (restless leg syndrome), and increased urges to gamble.

C   *Client background:* Bob reports learning to gamble as early as age 10 with neighbourhood kids his age. He reports playing cards for money every evening with his brother. His brother took him to the racetrack at the age of 15 and showed him how to bet. During his college years, he reports sports betting with his friends and others in the dorms. He said it was "just for fun." He would also sports-bet on the Internet but soon needed money in the account to continue gambling. He would switch between various betting sites depending on how much free play or match bet money he could get. He was currently working in the computer industry and found himself telling clients to make their checks out to his company name instead of the main computer company name. He then went to Las Vegas during March Madness and played the slots in between sports games. He placed a $5 bet and hit for a jackpot of $500,000. He spent the entire jackpot during his time in Las Vegas. [And you continue to articulate, in as much detail as possible, the gambling activities and behaviors showing the progression, compulsivity, and inability to cut down or stop.]

Previous treatment: Bob has never had any gambling-specific treatment, inpatient or outpatient. He reports receiving treatment by a psychiatrist for his anxiety and mood disorder symptoms. He has never attended 12-Step meetings, such as Gamblers Anonymous (GA). [Continue to expand on all mental health, substance-use disorder, and gambling treatment, including dates, level of care, and any medications that were prescribed.]

Family interview: Evaluator conducted phone interview with Bob's brother, on [date]. Brother reports his brother has been gambling as long as he can remember. He reports he would receive bailouts from their parents until he was in his early 30s. He reports that he never received gambling disorder specific treatment. [Conduct interviews with any family members that can comment on the gambling behaviour, as well as any earlier childhood behaviors that may demonstrate the predisposition and vulnerability to gambling.]

Clinical evaluation: Bob was interviewed on [date] at [location]. The interview lasted approximately two hours and employed several gambling-specific assessments and interviewing techniques that are typically used during a gambling-specific clinical assessment. At the beginning of the interview, Bob was administered the Mini-Mental Status Exam Mini-Mental Status Exam (MMSE) to establish baseline for his ability to participate in a lengthy interview. He was relaxed and engaged in the interview; speech was normal in tone and amount; mood was within normal limits; affect was full range; thought process was such that was able to answer questions without repeating them; thought content showed no current suicidal or homicidal ideation; no current hallucinations; cognition: alert; oriented, names and follows commands: 3/3 at 0 minutes and 3/3 at 5 minute recall; WORLD–DLROW; serial 7s to 79.

Lifetime South Oaks Gambling Screen (SOGS) score: 17 out of 20

Problem Gambling Severity Index (PGSI) score: 14—Severe Gambling Problem

DSM-5 Gambling Disorder: met 7 out of 9 (in bold)

1 **Need to gamble with increasing amounts of money in order to achieve the desired excitement**. Increasing bets with in-game betting on sports, and moving to "high limit slots" machines.

2 Is restless or irritable when attempting to cut down or stop gambling.

3 **Has made repeated unsuccessful efforts to control, cut back, or stop gambling**. "I don't know as I never set a limit for myself when I gambled."

4 **Is often preoccupied with gambling (e.g. having persistent thoughts of reliving past gamblilng experiences, handicapping or planning the next venture, thinking of ways to get money with which to gamble)**. "I was always looking at my work schedule to see how much money I could get from people during my insurance sales calls."

5 **Often gambles when feeling distressed (e.g. helpless, guilty, anxious, depressed)**. "I was in another world that felt focused."

6   **After losing money gambling, often returns another day to get even ("chasing one's losses).** "Won at sports at 11am, got my money, played slots, and stayed all night playing to get my money back. Stopped when I was broke."

7   **Lies to conceal the extent of involvement with gambling.** "I told lies everyday and didn't even try and remember what I said the day before."

8   Has jeopardized or lost a significant relationship, job, or educational or career opportunity because of gambling.

9   **Relies on others to provide money to relieve desperate financial situations caused by gambling**. "I had family and neighbors take out loans in their names, used all my credit on credit cards, and took advances from my employer."

Recommendations for treatment: Bob would benefit from gambling-specific treatment while incarcerated. Unfortunately, the Bureau of Prisons does not provide any gambling-specific treatment like substance-use disorder treatment. Bob would benefit from attending a dual diagnosis or SUD treatment program with emphasis on gambling as his primary drug of choice. It is not likely that federal treatment providers will be certified or trained in problem gambling so Bob will receive minimal psychoeducation and awareness about his gambling addiction while incarcerated. It is strongly recommended that he receive mandated treatment upon release or at the time for step-down in legal supervision. He would also benefit from self-excluding on the online and local gambling establishments but it would need to be voluntary.

Recovery: Recovery from gambling addiction includes periods of clean time without placing bets, attending self-help meetings, financial protection plan, family involvement, adherence to medication, and recovery from other addictions. Bob has not expressed or demonstrated any previous attempts to live a life of recovery. Bob will need to have his medication monitored closely to avoid receiving any medications that have FDA warnings for potential excessive gambling side-effects.

[Sign your name with your credentials; date]

Example Full Report to an Attorney on Behalf of Your Client

The following section is an example of what you can give to your client's attorney (per their request). You may need to include the initial report as discussed in this chapter. This will be determined by the requesting attorney. Include this additional information which can only be done when a client is receiving gambling specific treatment.

Treatment Outcomes

At the time of this report, Mr. X has accomplished the following treatment outcomes:

Treatment attendance: 25 sessions attended, 0 no-shows, 0 cancellations.

Medication management: PCP appointment on June 16, 20XX. Verification of medication refills from HSA transactions. Depression symptom improvement as measured by repeated BDI over time.

Financial budget: Completed initial and updates monthly with actual spending amounts. Verified by printed budget reports presented to therapist during sessions. Mr. X has been able to meet monthly expenses with current income without incurring additional debt.

Financial restitution plan: Making payments on all debts, including $250/month to mother towards $50,000 debt and $450/month towards school loan debt. Mr. X has also demonstrated meeting new financial obligations related to his medical/dental expenses without incurring further debt. These transactions have been verified by his therapist who reviewed Mr. X's online bank statement during the session.

Financial protection plan: Mr. X's mother changed the beneficiary on her life insurance policy to Mr. X's brother, in trust. Mr. X's sister has an online bank account login and password to review any and all transactions when desired. Mr. X's paycheck is automatically deposited into his bank account. Since May 3, Mr. X has not withdrawn cash (ATM) from his bank account for gambling as verified by his therapist review of an online bank statement.

Self-exclusion: Mr. X has self-excluded LIFETIME for PA (5/24/XX), OH (9/21/XX), and WV (9/21/XX). Verified by official paperwork reviewed during session with the therapist.

Gamblers Anonymous attendance: Weekly attendance since 6/14/XX and reports over 180 days clean since first meeting attendance. GA measures "clean days" from the first GA meeting attended. Also verified by letter written from a GA member on Mr. X's behalf.

Family involvement: Parents attended therapy session on 7/26/XX; brother via phone, and boyfriend attended Gamanon Meeting on 8/9/XX.

Celebrate Recovery: Mr. X began attending bi-weekly recovery meetings at a place of worship since 8/29/XX.

Employment: Mr. X is maintaining full-time employment. Mr. X received the highest rating on his Annual Performance Review. He also received a promotion in September. The store he manages exceeded the budget percentage for most dollars sold and highest increase in productivity.

Psychological testing: It is recommended that Mr. X receive a full psychological evaluation including testing to determine if any other disorders, impairments, or personality disorders are also present.

References

Achab, S. & Khazaal, Y. (2011). Psychopharmacological treatment in pathological gambling: A critical review. *Current Pharmaceutical Design, 17*(14), 1389–1395.

Alegría, A.A., Petry, N.M., Hasin, D.S., Liu, S. M., Grant, B. F., & Blanco, C. (2009). Disordered gambling among racial and ethnic groups in the US: Results from the National Epidemiologic Survey on Alcohol and Related Conditions. *CNS Spectrums, 14*(3), 132–143.

American Gaming Association (2019a). *Interactive map: Sports betting in the U.S.* Accessed on 05/20/20 at www.americangaming.org/research/state-gaming-map.

American Gaming Association (2019b). *State of the States*. Accessed on 05/20/20 at www.americangaming.org/wp-content/uploads/2019/06/AGA-2019-State-of-the-States_FINAL.pdf.

American Psychiatric Association (2013). *Diagnostic and Statistical Manual of Mental Disorders (5th ed.)*. Washington, DC: APA.

American Psychiatric Association (2018). *What is gambling disorder?* Accessed on 05/20/20 at www.psychiatry.org/patients-families/gambling-disorder/what-is-gambling-disorder.

Americans with Disabilities Act of 1990, Pub. L. No. 101-336, 104 Stat. 328 (1990).

Auer, M. & Griffiths, M.D. (2013). Voluntary limit setting and player choice in most intense online gamblers: An empirical study of gambling behaviour. *Journal of Gambling Studies, 29*(4), 647–660.

Auer, M.M. & Griffiths, M.D. (2015). The use of personalized behavioral feedback for online gamblers: An empirical study. *Frontiers in Psychology, 6*, 1406.

Baidawi, A. (2018). Australians are the world's biggest gambling losers, and some seek action. *The New York Times*, April 04. Accessed on 05/20/20 at. www.nytimes.com/2018/04/04/world/australia/australians-gambling-betting-machines.html.

Barrault, S. & Varescon, I. (2013). Cognitive distortions, anxiety, and depression among regular and pathological gambling online poker players. *Cyberpsychology, Behavior, and Social Networking, 16*(3), 183–188.

Beck, A.T., Ward, C.H., Mendelson, M., Mock, J., & Erbaugh, J. (1961). An inventory for measuring depression. *Archives of General Psychiatry, 4*, 561–571.

Bellegarde, J.D. & Potenza, M.R. (2010). Neurobiology of Pathological Gambling. In D. Ross, H. Kincaid, D. Spurrett, & P. Collins (eds), *What Is Addiction?* Cambridge, MA: MIT Press.

Benhsain, K., Taillefer, A., & Ladouceur, R. (2004). Awareness of independence of events and erroneous perceptions while gambling. *Addictive Behaviors*, *29*(2), 399–404.

Black, D.W., Shaw, M.C., McCormick, B.A., & Allen, J. (2012). Marital status, childhood maltreatment, and family dysfunction: A controlled study of pathological gambling. *The Journal of Clinical Psychiatry*, *73*(10), 1293–1297.

Blanco, C., Potenza, M.N., Kim, S.W., Ibáñez, A., Zaninelli, R., Saiz-Ruiz, J., & Grant, J.E. (2009). A pilot study of impulsivity and compulsivity in pathological gambling. Psychiatry Research, 167(1–2), 161–168.

Blaszczynski, A., Collins, P., Fong, D., Ladouceur, R., Nower, L., Shaffer, H., Tavares, H., & Venisse, J. L. (2011). Responsible gambling: General principles and minimal requirements. *Journal of Gambling Studies*, *27*, 565–573.

Blaszczynski, A. & Hunt, C. (2011). Online Sports Betting Has Created New Generation of Problem Gamblers. *Sydney: The University of Sydney.*

Blaszczynski, A., Gainsbury, S., & Karlov, L. (2014). Blue gum gaming machine: An evaluation of responsible gambling features. *Journal of Gambling Studies*, *30*(3), 697–712.

Blaszczynski, A., Ladouceur, R., & Nower, L. (2007). Self-exclusion: A proposed gateway to treatment model. *International Gambling Studies*, *7*(1), 59–71.

Blaszczynski, A. & Nower, L. (2002). A pathways model of problem and pathological gambling. *Addiction*, *97*(5), 487–499.

Boughton, R. & Falenchuk, O. (2007). Vulnerability and comorbidity factors of female problem gambling. *Journal of Gambling Studies*, *23*(3), 323–334.

Bowen, S., Chawla, N., Collins, S.E., Witkiewitz, K., *et al.* (2009). Mindfulness-based relapse prevention for substance use disorders: A pilot efficacy trial. *Substance Abuse*, *30*(4), 295–305.

Bowen, S., Chawla, N., & Marlatt, G.A. (2010). Mindfulness-Based Relapse Prevention for Addictive Behaviors: A Clinician's Guide. New York, NY: Guilford Press.

Braverman, J., LaPlante, D.A., Nelson, S.E., & Shaffer, H.J. (2013). Using cross-game behavioral markers for early identification of high-risk Internet gamblers. *Psychology of Addictive Behaviors*, *27*(3), 868–877.

Bringing Recovery Supports to Scale (2017). Peer Support. Accessed on 06/15/20 at www.samhsa.gov/sites/default/files/programs_campaigns/brss_tacs/peer-support-2017.pdf.

Broda, A., LaPlante, D.A., Nelson, S.E., LaBrie, R.A., Bosworth, L.B., & Shaffer, H.J. (2008). Virtual harm reduction efforts for Internet gambling: Effects of deposit limits on actual Internet sports gambling behavior. *Harm Reduction Journal*, *5*(1), 1–9.

Browne, B.R. (1994). Really not God: Secularization and pragmatism in Gamblers Anonymous. *Journal of Gambling Studies*, 10(3), 247–260.

Buffer (2019). *State of social.* Accessed on 05/20/20 at https://buffer.com/state-of-social-2019.

Busby, M. (2019). UK gambling-related hospital admissions up to more than one a day. The Guardian, December 24. Accessed on 05/20/20 at www.theguardian.com/society/2019/dec/24/uk-gambling-related-hospital-admissions-more-than-one-a-day.

Calado, F., Alexandre, J., & Griffiths, M.D. (2017). Prevalence of adolescent problem gambling: A systematic review of recent research. *Journal of Gambling Studies*, *33*(2), 397–424.

Calado, F. & Griffiths, M.D. (2016). Problem gambling worldwide: An update and systematic review of empirical research (2000–2015). *Journal of Behavioral Addictions*, *5*(4), 592–613.

Canale, N., Vieno, A., Griffiths, M.D., Marino, C., Chieco, F., Disperati, F., Andrioloa, S., & Santinello, M. (2016). The efficacy of a web-based gambling intervention program for high school students: A preliminary randomized study. *Computers in Human Behavior*, *55*, 946–954.

Celebrate Recovery (2018) Accessed on 05/20/20 at www.celebraterecovery.com.

Chamberlain, S.R., Derbyshire, K., Leppink, E., & Grant, J.E. (2015). Impact of ADHD symptoms on clinical and cognitive aspects of problem gambling. *Comprehensive Psychiatry, 57*, 51–57.

Chambless, D.L. & Ollendick, T.H. (2001). Empirically supported psychological interventions: Controversies and evidence. *Annual Review of Psychology, 52*(1), 685–716.

Champine, R.B. & Petry, N.M. (2010). Pathological gamblers respond equally well to cognitive-behavioral therapy regardless of other mental health treatment status. *The American Journal on Addictions, 19*(6), 550–556.

Chapman, S.L.C. & Wu, L.-T. (2012). Substance abuse among individuals with intellectual disabilities. *Research in Developmental Disabilities, 33*(4), 1147–1156.

Christensen, D.R., Dowling, N.A., Jackson, A.C., Brown, M., Russo, J., Francis, K.L., & Umemoto, A. (2013). A proof of concept for using brief dialectical behavior therapy as a treatment for problem gambling. *Behavior Change, 30*(2), 117–370.

Christensen, D.R., Witcher, C.S., Leighton, T., Hudson-Breen, R., & Ofori-Dei, S. (2018). Piloting the addition of contingency management to best practice counselling as an adjunct treatment for rural and remote disordered gamblers: Study protocol. *BMJ Open, 8*(4).

Ciarrocchi, J.W. (2001). *Counseling Problem Gamblers: A Self-Regulation Manual for Individual and Family Therapy.* Amsterdam: Elsevier.

Clements, J. (2019). *Internet usage worldwide – statistics and facts.* Statista. Accessed on 05/20/20 at www.statista.com/topics/1145/Internet-usage-worldwide.

Clotfelter, C.T. & Cook, P.J. (1993). The "gambler's fallacy" in lottery play. *Management Science, 39*(12), 1521–1525.

Constantino, J.N., Strom, S., Bunis, M., Nadler, C., *et al.* (2020). Toward actionable practice parameters for "dual diagnosis": Principles of assessment and management for co-occurring psychiatric and intellectual/developmental disability. *Current Psychiatry Reports, 22*(2), 9.

Cowlishaw, S., Merkouris, S., Dowling, N., Anderson, C., Jackson, A., & Thomas, S. (2012). Psychological therapies for pathological and problem gambling. *Cochrane Database of Systematic Reviews, 11*.

Crockett, M.J., Clark, L., & Robbins, T.W. (2009). Reconciling the role of serotonin in behavioral inhibition and aversion: Acute tryptophan depletion abolishes punishment-induced inhibition in humans. *The Journal of Neuroscience: The Official Journal of the Society for Neuroscience, 29*(38), 11993–11999.

Croson, R. & Sundali, J. (2005). The gambler's fallacy and the hot hand: Empirical data from casinos. *Journal of Risk and Uncertainty, 30*(3), 195–209.

Cunningham, J.A. (2005). Little use of treatment among problem gamblers. *Psychiatric Services, 56*(8), 1024–1025.

Cunningham-Williams, R.M., Cottler, L.B., Compton, W.M., Spitznagel, E.L., & Ben-Abdallah, A. (2000). Problem gambling and comorbid psychiatric and substance use disorders among drug users recruited from drug treatment and community settings. *Journal of Gambling Studies, 16*(4), 347–376.

de Lisle, S.M., Dowling, N.A., & Sabura Allen, J. (2011). Mindfulness-based cognitive therapy for problem gambling. *Clinical Case Studies, 10*(3), 210–228.

de Vogue, A. & Vazquez, M. (2018). Supreme Court lets states legalize sports gambling. *CNN Politics,* May 14. Accessed on 05/20/20 at https://edition.cnn.com/2018/05/14/politics/sports-betting-ncaa-supreme-court/index.html.

Delfabbro, P., Borgas, M., & King, D. (2012). Venue staff knowledge of their patrons' gambling and problem gambling. *Journal of Gambling Studies, 28*(2), 155–169.

Delfabbro, P.H., King, D.L., Lambos, C., & Puglies, S. (2009). Is video game playing a risk factor for pathological gambling in Australian adolescents? *Journal of Gambling Studies, 25*, 391–405.

Derevensky, J. & Gupta, R. (2004). Adolescents with gambling problems: A review of our current knowledge. *e-Gambling: The Electronic Journal of Gambling Issues, 10*, 119–140.

Desai, R.A. & Potenza, M.N. (2009). A cross sectional study of problem and pathological gambling in patients with schizophrenia/schizoaffective disorder. *The Journal of Clinical Psychiatry*, 70(9), 1250.

Dickerson, M., Hinchy, J., & Fabre, J. (1987). Chasing, arousal and sensation seeking in off-course gamblers. *British Journal of Addiction*, *82*(6), 673–680.

Dixon, M.R. (2000). Manipulating the illusion of control: Variations in gambling as a function of perceived control over chance outcomes. *The Psychological Record*, *50*(4), 705–719.

Dixon, M.R., Hayes, L.J., & Aban, I.B. (2000). Examining the roles of rule following, reinforcement, and preexperimental histories on risk-taking behavior. *The Psychological Record*, *50*, 687–704.

Dixon, M.R. & Wilson, A.N., (2014). *Acceptance and Commitment Therapy for Gambling Disorders*. Chicago, IL: Shawnee Scientific Press.

Dixon, M.R., Wilson, A.N., & Habib, R. (2016). Neurological evidence of acceptance and commitment therapy effectiveness in college-age gamblers. *Journal of Contextual Behavioral Science*, *5*(2), 80–88.

Dixon, M.R., Wilson, A.N., Belisle, J., & Schreiber, J.B. (2018). A functional analytic approach to understanding disordered gambling. *The Psychological Record*, *68*(2), 177–187.

Dragicevic, S., Percy, C., Kudic, A., & Parke, J. (2015). A descriptive analysis of demographic and behavioral data from Internet gamblers and those who self-exclude from online gambling platforms. *Journal of Gambling Studies*, *31*(1), 105–132.

Echeburúa, E., Fernández-Montalvo, J., & Báez, C. (2000). Relapse prevention in the treatment of slot-machine pathological gambling: Long-term outcome. *Behavior Therapy*, *31*(2), 351–364.

Economou, M., Souliotis, K., Mallori, M., Peppou, L.E., *et al.* (2019). Problem gambling in Greece: Prevalence and risk factors during the financial crisis. *Journal of Gambling Studies*, 1–18.

Edens, E. & Rosenheck, R. (2012). Rates and correlates of pathological gambling among VA mental health service users. *Journal of Gambling Studies, 28*, 1–11.

Ellenbogen, S., Derevensky, J., & Gupta, R. (2007). Gender differences among adolescents with gambling-related problems. *Journal of Gambling Studies, 23*, 133–143.

Ellenbogen, S., Gupta, R., & Derevensky, J.L. (2007). A cross-cultural study of gambling behaviour among adolescents. *Journal of Gambling Studies*, *23*(1), 25–39.

Estevez, A., Rodriguez, R., Diaz, N., Granero, R., *et al.* (2017). How do online sports gambling disorder patients compare with land-based patients? *Journal of Behavioral Addictions*, *6*(4), 639–647.

European Gaming & Betting Association (2018). *EU Market*. Accessed on 05/20/20 at www.egba.eu/eu-market.

Ferris, J. & Wynne, H. (2001). *The Canadian Problem Gambling Index: Final Report*. Ottawa: Canadian Centre on Substance Abuse.

Fong, T.W. (2005). Types of psychotherapy for pathological gamblers. *Psychiatry (Edgmont)*, *2*(5), 32.

Fortune, E.E. & Goodie, A.S. (2012). Cognitive distortions as a component and treatment focus of pathological gambling: A review. *Psychology of Addictive Behaviors*, *2*, 298–310.

Freeman, J.R., Volberg, R.A., & Zorn, M. (2020). Correlates of at-risk and problem gambling among veterans in Massachusetts. *Journal of Gambling Studies*, *36*(1), 69–83.

Gainsbury, S.M., King, D.L., Russell, A.M.T., Delfabbro, P., Derevensky, J., & Hing, N. (2016). Exposure to and engagement with gambling marketing in social media: Reported impacts on moderate-risk and problem gamblers. *Psychology of Addictive Behaviors, 30*(2), 270–276.

Gainsbury, S.M., Russell, A., & Hing, N. (2014). An investigation of social casino gaming among land-based and Internet gamblers: A comparison of socio-demographic characteristics, gambling and co-morbidities. *Computers in Human Behavior, 33*, 126–135.

Gainsbury, S., Aro, D., Ball, D., Tobar, C., & Russell, A. (2015). Determining optimal placement for pop-up messages: Evaluation of a live trial of dynamic warning messages for electronic gaming machines. *International Gambling Studies, 15*(1), 141–158.

Gainsbury, S.M., Russell, A., Hing, N., Wood, R., & Blaszczynski, A. (2013). The impact of Internet gambling on gambling problems: A comparison of moderate-risk and problem Internet and non-Internet gamblers. *Psychology of Addictive Behaviors, 27*(4), 1092–1101.

Gainsbury, S.M., Suhonen, N., & Saastamoinen, J. (2014). Chasing losses in online poker and casino games: Characteristics and game play of Internet gamblers at risk of disordered gambling. *Psychiatry Research, 217*(3), 220–225.

Gambino, B. & Lesieur, H. (2006). The South Oaks Gambling Screen (SOGS): A rebuttal to critics. *Journal of Gambling Issues, 17*, 1–16

Gamblers Anonymous (2000). *GA: A New Beginning*. Gamblers Anonymous International Service Office.

Gambling Act (2005). c. 19. www.legislation.gov.uk/ukpga/2005/19/section/4.

Gambling Commission. (2019). Industry statistics: April 2016 to March 2019. Accessed on 05/20/20 at www.gamblingcommission.gov.uk/PDF/survey-data/Gambling-industry-statistics.pdf.

Gavriel-Fried, B., Moretta, T., & Potenza, M.N. (2020). Associations between recovery capital, spirituality, and DSM–5 symptom improvement in gambling disorder. *Psychology of Addictive Behaviors, 34*(1), 209–217.

Gebauer, L., LaBrie, R., & Shaffer, H.J. (2010). Optimizing DSM-IV-TR classification accuracy: A brief biosocial screen for detecting current gambling disorders among gamblers in the general household population. *Canadian Journal of Psychiatry. Revue Canadienne De Psychiatrie, 55*(2), 82–90.

Gerstein, D.R., Murphy, S.A., Toce, M.T., Hoffman, J., *et al.* (1999). *Gambling impact and behavior study: Report to the National Gambling Impact Study Commission*. Chicago, IL: National Opinion Research Center.

Gilsenan, K. (2019). *2019 in review: Social media is changing, and it's not a bad thing.* GlobalWebIndex. Accessed on 05/20/20 at https://blog.globalwebindex.com/trends/2019-in-review-social-media.

Giovanni, M., Fabiola, S., Federica, F., Mariangela, C., *et al.* (2017). An overview of the associated co-morbidity and clinical characteristics. *International Journal of High Risk Behaviors and Addiction, 6*(3), e30827.

Glassford, T.S., Wilson, A.N., & Gupta, V. (2020). Risky Business: Increasing risky betting through rule-governed behavior. *The Analysis of Verbal Behavior, 36*, 146–156.

Global Fire Power (2020). *2020 Military Strength Ranking*. Accessed on 05/20/20 at www.global-firepower.com/countries-listing.asp.

Gonzalez-Ibanex, A., Rosel, P., & Moreno, I. (2005). Evaluation and treatment of pathological gambling. *Journal of Gambling Studies, 21*, 35–42.

Goudriaan, A.E. (2011). Brain imaging studies: A review. *Increasing The Odds: A Series Dedicated to Understanding Gambling Disorders, 6*, 14–19.

Grant, J.E., Brewer, J.A., & Potenza, M.N. (2006). The neurobiology of substance and behavioral addictions. *CNS Spectrums, 11*(12), 924–930.

Grant, J.E., Donahue, C.B., Odlaug, B.L., & Kim, S.W. (2011). A 6-month follow-up of imaginal desensitization plus motivational interviewing in the treatment of pathological gambling. *Annals of Clinical Psychiatry: Official Journal of the American Academy of Clinical Psychiatrists, 23*(1), 3–10.

Grant, J., Donahue, C., Odlaug, B., Kim, S., Miller, M., & Petry, N. (2009). Imaginal desensitisation plus motivational interviewing for pathological gambling: Randomised controlled trial. *The British Journal of Psychiatry, 195*(3), 266–267.

Grant J.E., Leppink, E.W., Redden, S.A., Odlaug, B.L., & Chamberlain, S.R. (2015). COMT genotype, gambling activity, and cognition. *Journal of Psychiatric Research, 68,* 371–376.

Grant, J.E. & Potenza, M.N. (2005). Tobacco use and pathological gambling. *Annals of Clinical Psychiatry, 17*(4), 237–241.

Grant, S., Colaiaco, B., Motala, A., Shanman, R., Booth, M., Sorbero, M., & Hempel, S. (2017). Mindfulness-based relapse prevention for substance use disorders: A systematic review and meta-analysis. *Journal of Addiction Medicine, 11*(5), 386–396.

Gray, A. (2019). The Vegas era: Major sports betting legislation in the USA (Part II). *Sports Betting Dime.* Accessed on 05/20/20 at www.sportsbettingdime.com/guides/legal/sports-betting-history-part-ii.

Gray, H.M., LaPlante, D.A., & Shaffer, H.J. (2012). Behavioral characteristics of Internet gamblers who trigger corporate responsible gambling interventions. *Psychology of Addictive Behaviors, 26*(3), 527–535.

Greene, R.R. (2008). Human Behavior Theory, Person-in-Environment, and Social Work Method. In R.R. Greene (ed.), *Human Behavior Theory and Social Work Practice (3rd ed.).* Piscataway, NJ: Transaction Publishers.

Grichting, W.L. (1986). The impact of religion on gambling in Australia. *Australian Journal of Psychology, 38*(1), 45–58.

Griffiths, M.D. & Barnes, A. (2008). Internet gambling: An online empirical study among student gamblers. *International Journal of Mental Health and Addiction, 6,* 194–204.

Griffiths, M.D., Shonin, E., & Van Gordon, W. (2016). Mindfulness as a treatment for gambling disorder: Current directions and issues. *Journal of Gambling and Commercial Gaming Research, 1*(1), 47–52.

Griffiths, M.D., Wardle, H., Orford, J., Sproston, K., & Erens, B. (2009). Sociodemographic correlates of Internet gambling: Findings from the 2007 British Gambling Prevalence Survey. *Cyberpsychology, Behavior, and Social Networking. 12,* 199–202.

Griffiths, M. & Wood, R.T.A. (2000). Risk factors in adolescence: The case of gambling, videogame playing, and the Internet. *Journal of Gambling Studies, 16,* 199–225.

Griffiths, M.D. & Whitty, M.W. (2010). Online behavioural tracking in Internet gambling research: Ethical and methodological issues. *International Journal of Internet Research Ethics, 3,* 104–117.

Guercio, J.M., Johnson, T., & Dixon, M.R. (2012). Behavioral treatment for pathological gambling in persons with acquired brain injury. *Journal of Applied Behavior Analysis, 45*(3), 485–495.

Gupta, R. & Derevensky, J.L. (1997). Familial and social influences on juvenile gambling behavior. *Journal of Gambling Studies, 13,* 179–192.

Gupta, R. & Derevensky, J.L. (2000a). Adolescents with gambling problems: From research to treatment. *Journal of Gambling Studies, 16*(2–3), 315–342.

Gupta, R. & Derevensky, J.L. (2000b). Preface/Editorial for the Special Issue. *Journal of Gambling Studies, 16*, 115–117.

Gyollai, Á., Griffiths, M.D., Barta, C., Vereczkei, A., *et al.* (2014). The genetics of problem and pathological gambling: A systematic review. *Current Pharmaceutical Design, 20*(25), 3993–3999.

Habib, R. & Dixon, M.R. (2010). Neurobehavioral evidence for the "near-miss" effect in pathological gamblers. *Journal of the Experimental Analysis of Behavior, 93*(3), 313–328.

Harm (2019). In *Merriam-Webster.com*. Accessed on 12/24/19 at www.merriam-webster.com/dictionary/harm.

Harris, A. & Griffiths, M.D. (2016). A critical review of the harm minimization tools available for electronic gambling. *Journal of Gambling Studies, 33*, 187–221.

Hayer, T. & Meyer, G. (2010). Internet self-exclusion: Characteristics of self-excluded gamblers and preliminary evidence for its effectiveness. *International Journal of Mental Health and Addiction, 9*, 296–307.

Hayes, S.C. (2004). Acceptance and commitment therapy, relational frame theory, and the third wave of behavioral and cognitive therapies. *Behavior Therapy, 35*, 639–665.

Hayes, S.C., Strosahl, K.D. & Wilson, K.G. (1999/2011) *Acceptance and Commitment Therapy: An Experiential Approach to Behavior Change.* New York, NY: Guilford Press.

He, W., Goodkind, D., & Kowal, P. (2015). *An Aging World: 2015.* United States Census Bureau. Accessed on 05/21/20 at www.census.gov/content/dam/Census/library/publications/2016/demo/p95-16-1.pdf.

Headway: The Brain Injury Association (2020). *The perils of gambling after brain injury. Brain injury and me.* Accessed on 05/21/20 at www.headway.org.uk/about-brain-injury/individuals/brain-injury-and-me/the-perils-of-gambling-after-brain-injury.

Hing, N. & Nuske, E. (2012). Responding to problem gamblers in the venue: Role conflict, role ambiguity, and challenges for hospitality staff. *Journal of Human Resources in Hospitality & Tourism, 11*(2), 146–164.

Hing, N., Russell, A.M., & Browne, M. (2017). Risk factors for gambling problems on online electronic gaming machines, race betting and sports betting. *Frontiers in Psychology, 8*, 779.

HM Revenue & Customs (2019). UK Betting and Gaming Statistics. Accessed on 05/21/20 at https://assets.publishing.service.gov.uk/government/uploads/system/uploads/attachment_data/file/843175/2019_Sep_Bet_and_Gam_Comm.pdf.

Hodgins, D.C., Currie, S.R., Currie, G., & Fick, G.H. (2009). Randomized trial of brief motivational treatments for pathological gamblers: More is not necessarily better. *Journal of Consulting and Clinical Psychology, 77*(5), 950–960.

Hodgins, D. & Diskin, K.M. (2008). Motivational Interviewing in the Treatment of Problem and Pathological Gambling. In H. Arkowitz, S. Rollnick, & W.R. Miller (eds), *Motivational Interviewing in the Treatment of Psychological Problems.* New York, NY: The Guilford Press.

Hodgins, D.C., Schopflocher, D.P., el-Guebaly, N., Casey, D.M., Smith, G.J., Williams, R.J., & Wood, R.T. (2010). The association between childhood maltreatment and gambling problems in a community sample of adult men and women. *Psychology of Addictive Behaviors, 24*(3), 548.

Holtgraves, T. (2009). Evaluating the problem gambling severity index. *Journal of Gambling Studies, 25*, 105–120.

Hong, J. (2019). Southeast Asia pulls back on online gambling as China rages. *Bloomberg*, August 19. Accessed on 05/21/20 at www.bloomberg.com/news/articles/2019-08-19/southeast-asia-pulls-back-on-online-gambling-as-china-rages.

HRSA Center for Integrated Health Solutions (2020). *Trauma*. Substance Abuse and Mental Health Services Administration. Accessed on 05/21/20 at www.integration.samhsa.gov/clinical-practice/trauma.

Huettel, S.A., Song, A.W., & McCarthy, G. (eds) (2009). *Functional Magnetic Resonance Imaging*. Massachusetts: Sinauer Associates.

Imperatori, C., Innamorati, M., Bersani, F.S., Imbimbo, F., Pompili, M., Contardi, A., & Farina, B. (2017). The association among childhood trauma, pathological dissociation and gambling severity in casino gamblers. *Clinical Psychology & Psychotherapy, 24*(1), 203–211.

Jacobs, D.F. (2000). Juvenile gambling in North America: An analysis of long term trends and future prospects. *Journal of Gambling Studies, 16,* 119–152.

Jacobs, D.F. (2004). Youth Gambling in North America: Long-term Trends and Future Prospects. In J.L. Derevensky & R. Gupta (eds) *Gambling Problems in Youth: Theoretical and Applied Perspectives*. New York, NY: Klewer Academic/Plenum Publishers.

Jiménez-Murcia, S., Alvarez-Moya, E.M., Stinchfield, R., Fernández-Aranda, F., *et al.* (2010). Age of onset in pathological gambling: Clinical, therapeutic and personality correlates. *Journal of Gambling Studies, 26*(2), 235–248.

Johnson, E.E., Hamer, R., Nora, R.M., Tan, B., Eistenstein, N., & Englehart, C. (1988). The lie/bet questionnaire for screening pathological gamblers. *Psychological Reports, 80*, 83–88.

Jordan, M.R. & Morgan, O. (eds) (2012). *Addiction and Spirituality: A Multidisciplinary Approach*. Nashville, TN: Chalice Press.

Karlsson, J., Broman, N., & Håkansson, A. (2019). Associations between problematic gambling, gaming, and Internet use: A cross-sectional population survey. *Journal of Addiction 2019*.

Katerndahl, D.A. (2008). Impact of spiritual symptoms and their interactions on health services and life satisfaction. *Annals of Family Medicine, 6*(5), 412–420.

Kausch, O., Rugle, L., & Rowland, D.Y. (2006). Lifetime histories of trauma among pathological gamblers. *The American Journal on Addictions, 15*(1), 35–43.

Kendall, P.C. & Hollon, S.D. (1979). Cognitive-Behavioral Interventions: Overview and Current Status. In P.C. Kendall & S.D. Hollon (eds), *Cognitive-Behavioral Interventions: Theory, Research, and Procedures*. New York, NY: Academic Press.

Kennedy, C.H., Cook, J.H., Poole, D.R., Brunson, C.L., & Jones, D.E. (2005). Review of the first year of an overseas military gambling treatment program. *Military Medicine, 170*(8), 683–687.

Kessler, R.C., Hwang, I., Labrie, R., Petukhova, M., Sampson, N.A., Winters, K.C., & Shaffer, H.J. (2008). DSM-IV pathological gambling in the National Comorbidity Survey Replication. *Psychological Medicine: A Journal of Research in Psychiatry and the Allied Sciences, 38*(9), 1351–1360.

Kitson, A., Harvey, G., & McCormack, B. (1998). Enabling the implementation of evidence-based practice: A conceptual framework. *BMJ Quality & Safety, 7*(3), 149–158.

Kraus, S.W., Etuk, R., & Potenza, M.N. (2020). Current pharmacotherapy for gambling disorder: A systematic review. *Expert Opinion on Pharmacotherapy*, 1–10.

Kroenke, K., Spitzer, R.L., & Williams, J.B. (2001). The PHQ-9: Validity of a brief depression severity measure. *Journal of General Internal Medicine, 16*(9), 606–613.

Kurtz, E. (1986). Origins of AA spirituality. *Blue Book, 38*, 35–42.

King, D.L., Gainsbury, S.M., Delfabbro, P.H., Hing, N., & Abarbanel, B. (2015). Distinguishing between gaming and gambling activities in addiction research. *Journal of Behavioral Addictions, 4*, 215.

LaBrie, R.A., Nelson, S.E., LaPlante, D.A., Peller, A.J., Caro, G., & Shaffer, H.J. (2007). Missouri casino self-excluders: Distributions across time and space. *Journal of Gambling Studies*, *23*(2), 231–243.

Ladouceur, R. & Lachance, S. (2007) *Overcoming Pathological Gambling*. Oxford: Oxford University Press.

Ladouceur, R., Boisvert, J.M., Pépin, M., Loranger, M., & Sylvain, C. (1994). Social cost of pathological gambling. *Journal of Gambling Studies*, *10*(4), 399–409.

Ladouceur, R., Gosselin, P., Laberge, M., & Blaszczynski, A. (2001). Dropouts in clinical research: Do results reported in the field of addiction reflect clinical reality? *The Behavior Therapist*, *24*, 44–46.

Ladouceur, R., Jacques, C., Giroux, I., Ferland, F., & Leblond, J. (2000). Analysis of a casino's self-exclusion program. *Journal of Gambling Studies*, *4*, 453–460.

Ladouceur, R., Lachance, S., & Fournier, P.-M. (2009). Is control a viable goal in the treatment of pathological gambling? *Behaviour Research and Therapy*, *47*(3), 189–197.

Ladouceur, R., Shaffer, P., Blaszczynski, A., & Shaffer, H. J. (2017). Responsible gambling: A synthesis of the empirical evidence. *Addiction Research & Theory*, *25*(3), 225–235.

Ladouceur, R., Sylvian, C., Boutin, C., & Doucet, C. (2002). *Understanding and Treating the Pathological Gambler*. West Sussex, England: John Wiley & Sons.

Ladouceur, R., Sylvian, C., Boutin, C., Lachance, S., Doucet, C., & Leblond, J. (2003). Group therapy for pathological gamblers: A cognitive approach. *Behaviour Research and Therapy*, *41*(5), 587–596.

Ladouceur, R., Sylvain, C., & Gosselin, P. (2007). Self-exclusion program: A longitudinal evaluation study. *Journal of Gambling Studies*, *23*(1), 85–94.

Ladouceur, R., Sylvain, C., Boutin, C., Lachance, S., Doucet, C., Leblond, J., & Jacques, C. (2001). Cognitive treatment of pathological gambling. *Journal of Nervous and Mental Disease*, 189, 766–773.

Ladouceur, R., Sylvain, C., Letarte, H., Giroux, I., & Jacques, C. (1998). Cognitive treatment of pathological gamblers. *Behaviour Research and Therapy*, *36*(12), 1111–1119.

Lahti, T., Halme, J.T., Pankakoski, M., Sinclair, D., & Alho, H. (2010). Treatment of pathological gambling with naltrexone pharmacotherapy and brief intervention: A pilot study. *Psychopharmacology Bulletin*, *43*(3), 35–44.

Langer, E.J. (1975). The illusion of control. *Journal of Personality and Social Psychology*, *32*(2), 311–328.

LaPlante, D.A., Gray, H.M., LaBrie, R.A., Kleschinsky, J.H., & Shaffer, H.J. (2012). Gaming industry employees' responses to responsible gambling training: A public health imperative. *Journal of Gambling Studies*, *28*(2), 171–191.

Larimer, M.E., Neighbors, C., Lostutter, T.W., Whiteside, U., Cronce, J.M., Kaysen, D. & Walker, D.D. (2012). Brief motivational feedback and cognitive behavioral interventions for prevention of disordered gambling: A randomized clinical trial. *Addiction*, *107*(6), 1148–1158.

Ledgerwood, D. & Milosevic, A. (2015). Clinical and personality characteristics associated with post-traumatic stress disorder in problem and pathological gamblers recruited from the community. *Journal of Gambling Studies*, *31*(2), 501–512.

Ledgerwood, D.M. & Petry, N.M. (2006). Posttraumatic stress disorder symptoms in treatment-seeking pathological gamblers. *Journal of Traumatic Stress*, *19*, 411–416.

Legal US online gambling guide (2020). Play USA. Accessed on 05/21/20 at www.playusa.com/us.

Lesieur, H.R. & Blume, S.B. (1987). The South Oaks Gambling Screen (SOGS): A new instrument for the identification of pathological gamblers. *The American Journal of Psychiatry, 144*(9), 1184–1188.

Lister, J.J., Milosevic, A., & Ledgerwood, D.M. (2015). Psychological characteristics of problem gamblers with and without mood disorder. *The Canadian Journal of Psychiatry, 60*(8), 369–376.

Lobsinger, C. & Beckett, L. (1996). *Odd on the Break Even. A Practical Approach to Gambling Awareness.* Canberra: Relationships Australia, Inc.

Logothetis, N.K. (2008). What we can do and what we cannot do with fMRI. *Nature, 453*(12), 869–878.

Luquiens, A., Lagadec, M., Tanguy, M., & Reynaud, M. (2015). Efficacy of online psychotherapies in poker gambling disorder: An online randomized clinical trial. *European Psychiatry, 30,* 1053.

Lyfe Marketing (2019) 32 social media market statistics that will change the way you think about social media. Accessed on 05/19/20 at www.lyfemarketing.com/blog/social-media-marketing-statistics.

Maclin, O.H., Dixon, M.R., & Hayes, L.J. (1999). A computerized slot machine simulation to investigate the variables involved in gambling behavior. *Behavior Research Methods, Instruments & Computers, 31*(4), 731–734.

Magnusson, K., Nilsson, A., Andersson, G., Hellner, C., & Carlbring, P. (2019). Internet-delivered cognitive-behavioral therapy for significant others of treatment-refusing problem gamblers: A randomized wait-list controlled trial. *Journal of Consulting and Clinical Psychology, 87*(9), 802–814.

Magoon, M.E. & Ingersoll, G.M. (2006). Parental modeling, attachment, and supervision as moderators of adolescent gambling. *Journal of Gambling Studies, 22*(1), 1–22.

Maier, N.R.F. (1930). Reasoning in humans. I. On direction. *Journal of Comparative Psychology, 10*(2), 115–143.

Market.us. (2019). *Social media statistics and facts.* Accessed on 05/21/20 at https://market.us/statistics/social-media.

Marlatt, G.A. & Gordon, J. (1985). *Relapse Prevention: Maintenance Strategies in the Treatment of Addictive Behaviours.* New York, NY: The Guilford Press.

Marshall, G.N., Elliott, M.N. & Schell, T.L. (2009). Prevalence and correlates of lifetime gambling in Cambodian refugees residing in Long Beach, CA. *Journal of Immigrant and Minority Health, 11*(1), 35–40.

Martinez, F., Le Floch, V., Gaffié, B., & Villejoubert, G. (2011). Reports of wins and risk taking: An investigation of the mediating effect of the illusion of control. *Journal of Gambling Studies, 27*(2), 271–285.

Matthieu, M.M., Wilson, A. & Casner, R.W. (2017). Interdisciplinary issues at the intersection of assessing and treating substance use disorders and post-traumatic stress disorder: Clinical social work and clinical behavioral analysis with veterans. *Advances in Social Work, 18*(1), 217–234.

Maynard, B.R., Wilson, A.N., Labuzienski, E., & Whiting, S.W. (2018). Mindfulness-based approaches in the treatment of disordered gambling: A systematic review and meta-analysis. *Research on Social Work Practice, 28*(3), 348–362.

McGoldrick, M., Gerson, R., & Shellenberger, S. (1999). *Genograms in Family Assessment. 2nd edition.* New York, NY: W.W. Norton & Company.

McKinlay, W.W., Brooks, D.N., Bond, M.R., Martinage, D.P., & Marshall, M.M. (1981). The short-term outcome of severe blunt head injury as reported by relatives of the injured persons. *Journal of Neurology, Neurosurgery, and Psychiatry, 44*(6), 527–533.

McNeilly, D.P. & Burke, W.J. (2000). Late life gambling: The attitudes and behaviors of older adults. *Journal of Gambling Studies, 16*(4), 393–415.

Medeiros, G.C. & Grant, J.E. (2019). Pharmacological Interventions in Gambling Disorder. In A. Heinz, N. Romanczuk-Seiferth, & M.N. Potenza (eds), *Gambling Disorder*. New York, NY: Springer, Cham.

Miller, L., Bansal, R., Wickramaratne, P., Hao, X., Tenke, C.E., Weissman, M.M., & Peterson, B.S. (2014). Neuroanatomical correlates of religiosity and spirituality: A study in adults at high and low familial risk for depression. *JAMA Psychiatry, 71*(2), 128–135.

Miller W.R. & Rollnick, S. (2012). *Motivational Interviewing: Helping People Change*. New York, NY: Guilford Press.

Milosevic, A. & Ledgerwood, D.M. (2010). The subtyping of pathological gambling: A comprehensive review. *Clinical Psychology Review, 30*(8), 988–998.

Moeller, F.G., Barratt, E.S., Dougherty, D.M., Schmitz, J.M., & Swann, M.D. (2001). Psychiatric aspects of impulsivity. *American Journal of Psychiatry: Official Journal of the American Psychiatric Association, 11*, 1783.

Moon, M., Lister, J.J., Milosevic, A., & Ledgerwood, D.M. (2017). Subtyping non-treatment-seeking problem gamblers using the pathways model. *Journal of Gambling Studies, 33*(3), 841–853.

Moore, T.J., Glenmullen, J., & Mattison, D.R. (2014). Reports of pathological gambling, hypersexuality, and compulsive shopping associated with dopamine receptor agonist drugs. *JAMA Internal Medicine, 174*(12), 1930–1933.

Muñoz, Y., Chebat, J.C. & Borges, A. (2013). Graphic gambling warnings: How they affect emotions, cognitive responses and attitude change. *Journal of Gambling Studies, 29*(3), 507–524.

Nastally, B.L. & Dixon, M.R. (2012). The effect of a brief acceptance and commitment therapy intervention on the near-miss effect in problem gamblers. *Psychological Record, 62*, 677–690.

National Council on Problem Gambling. (2019). *Internet Responsible Gambling Standards*. Accessed on 05/21/20 at www.ncpgambling.org/wp-content/uploads/2019/10/NCPG-IRGS-FINAL.pdf.

National Endowment for Financial Education (2000). *Personal financial strategies for the loved ones of problem gamblers*. Accessed on 05/21/20 at www.ncpgambling.org/wp-content/uploads/2014/08/loved_ones_guide_ncpg_booklet.pdf.

National Institute of Justice (2004). *Gambling and crime among arrestees: Exploring the link*. Research for Practice. Accessed on 05/21/20 at www.ncjrs.gov/pdffiles1/nij/203197.pdf.

Nelson, S.E., Kleschinsky, J.H., LaBrie, R.A., Kaplan, S., & Shaffer, H.J. (2010). One decade of self exclusion: Missouri casino self-excluders four to ten years after enrollment. *Journal of Gambling Studies, 26*(1), 129–144.

Nelson, S.E., LaPlante, D.A., Peller, A.J., Schumann, A., LaBrie., R.A., & Shaffer, H.J. (2008). Real limits in the virtual world: Self-limiting behavior of Internet gamblers. *Journal of Gambling Studies, 24*(4), 463–477.

Nevo, I. & Slonim-Nevo, V. (2011). The myth of evidence-based practice: Towards evidence-informed practice. *British Journal of Social Work, 41*(6), 1176–1197.

Newhouse, E. (2013). Vets vulnerable to gambling addictions. *Psychology Today*. Accessed on 05/21/20 at www.psychologytoday.com/us/blog/invisible-wounds/201305/vets-vulnerable-gambling-addictions.

Nilsson, A., Magnusson, K., Carlbring, P., Andersson, G., & Gumpert, C.H. (2018). The development of an Internet-based treatment for problem gamblers and concerned significant others: A pilot randomized controlled trial. *Journal of Gambling Studies, 2*, 539–559.

Nower, L. & Blaszczynski, A. (2004). The pathways model as harm minimization for youth gamblers in educational settings. *Child and Adolescent Social Work Journal, 21*(1), 25–45.

Nower, L.M. & Blaszczynski, A.P. (2006). Characteristics and gender differences among self-excluded casino problem gamblers: Missouri data. *Journal of Gambling Studies, 22*(1), 81–99.

Nower, L. & Blaszczynski, A. (2017). Development and validation of the Gambling Pathways Questionnaire (GPQ). *Psychology of Addictive Behaviors, 31*(1), 95.

O'Neill, K. (2017). Relapse Prevention in Problem Gambling. In C. McIntosh & K. O'Neill (eds), *Evidence-Based Treatments for Problem Gambling*. New York, NY: Springer, Cham.

Oei, T.P., Raylu, N., & Casey, L.M. (2010). Effectiveness of group and individual formats of a combined motivational interviewing and cognitive behavioral treatment program for problem gambling: A randomized controlled trial. *Behavioural and Cognitive Psychotherapy, 38*(2), 233–238.

Okuda, M., Balán, I., Petry, N.M., Oquendo, M., & Blanco, C. (2009). Cognitive-behavioral therapy for pathological gambling: Cultural considerations. *American Journal of Psychiatry, 166*(12), 1325–1330.

Orman, S. (2010). *Women and Money: Owning the Power to Control Your Destiny*. New York, NY: Spiegel & Grau.

PBS Newshour (2019). How social casinos use Facebook to target the vulnerable. *PBS*. Accessed on 05/21/20 at www.pbs.org/video/risky-bets-1565730682.

Peers. (n.d.). Accessed on 06/15/20 at www.samhsa.gov/brss-tacs/recovery-support-tools/peers.

Peter, S.C., Whelan, J.P., Ginley, M.K., Pfund, R.A., Wilson, K.K., & Meyers, A.W. (2016). Disordered gamblers with and without ADHD: The role of coping in elevated psychological distress. *International Gambling Studies, 16*(3), 455–469.

Petry, N.M. (2001). Pathological gamblers, with and without substance use disorders, discount delayed rewards at high rates. *Journal of Abnormal Psychology, 110*(3), 482–487.

Petry, N.M. (2005). *Pathological Gambling: Etiology, Comorbidity, and Treatment*. Washington, DC: American Psychological Association.

Petry, N.M. (2010). Contingency management treatments: Controversies and challenges. *Addiction, 105*, 1507–1509.

Petry, N.M., Armentano, C., Kuoch, T., Norinth, T., & Smith, L. (2003). Gambling participation and problems among South East Asian refugees to the United States. *Psychiatric Services, 54*(8), 1142–1148.

Petry, N.M., Kolodner, K.B., Li, R., Peirce, J.M., Roll, J.M., Stitzer, M.L., & Hamilton, J.A. (2006). Prize-based contingency management does not increase gambling. *Drug and Alcohol Dependency, 83*(3), 269–273.

Petry, N.M. & Steinberg, K.L. (2005). Childhood maltreatment in male and female treatment-seeking pathological gamblers. *Psychology of Addictive Behaviors, 19*, 226–229.

Petry, N.M., Weinstock, J., Ledgerwood, D.M., & Morasco, B. (2008). A randomized trial of brief interventions for problem and pathological gamblers. *Journal of Consulting and Clinical Psychology, 76*(2), 318–328.

Petry, N.M., Weinstock, J., Morasco, B.J., & Ledgerwood, D.M. (2009). Brief motivational interventions for college student problem gamblers. *Addiction, 104*(9), 1569–1578.

Pew Research Center (2019). *Defining generations: Where Millennials and Generation Z begins.* FactTank. Accessed on 05/21/20 at www.pewresearch.org/fact-tank/2019/01/17/where-millennials-end-and-generation-z-begins.

Pfund, R.A., Peter, S.C., Whelan, J.P., Meyers, A.W., Ginley, M.K., & Relyea, G. (2020). Is more better? A meta-analysis of dose and efficacy in face-to-face psychological treatments for problem and disordered gambling. *Psychology of Addictive Behaviors.* Advance online publication. http://dx.doi.org/10.1037/adb0000560.

Portney, L.G. (2020). *Foundations of Clinical Research: Applications to Evidence-Based Practice.* Philadelphia, PA: F.A. Davis Company.

Potenza, M.N. (2006). Should addictive disorders include nonsubstance-related conditions? *Addiction 101 (Suppl. 1),* 142–151.

Potenza, M.N. (2007). Impulsivity and compulsivity in pathological gambling and obsessive-compulsive disorder. *Revista Brasileira de Psiquiatrai, 29,* 105–106.

Potenza, M.N. (2008). The neurobiology of pathological gambling and drug addiction: An overview and new findings. *Philosophical Transactions: Biological Sciences, 363*(1507), 3181–3189.

Potenza, M.N., Leung, H., Blumberg, H.P., Peterson, B.S., Fulbright, R.K., Lacadie, C.M., Skudlarski, P., & Gore, J.C. (2003). An fMRI stroop task study on ventromedial prefrontal cortical function in pathological gamblers. *American Journal of Psychiatry, 160*(11), 1990–1994.

Potenza, M.N., Steinberg, M.A., Skudlarski, P., Fulbright, R.K., *et al.* (2003). Gambling urges in pathological gambling: A functional magnetic resonance imaging study. *Archives of General Psychiatry, 60*(8), 828–836.

Potenza, M.N., Voon, V., & Weintraub, D. (2007). Drug Insight: Impulse control disorders and dopamine therapies in Parkinson's disease. *Nature Clinical Practice Neurology, 3*(12), 664–672.

Prendergast, M., Podus, D., Finney, J., Greenwell, L., & Roll, J. (2006). Contingency management for treatment of substance use disorders: A meta-analysis. *Addiction, 101*(11), 1546–1560.

Prochaska, J.O. & Velicer, W.F. (1997). The transtheoretical model of health behavior change. *American Journal of Health Promotion, 12,* 38–48.

Queensland Government Statistician's Office (2019). *Australian gambling statistics, 35th edition.* Accessed on 05/21/20 at www.qgso.qld.gov.au/issues/2646/australian-gambling-statistics-35th-edn-1992-93-2017-18.pdf.

Rahman, A.S., Pilver, C.E., Desai, R.A., Steinberg, M.A., Rugle, L., Krishnan-Sarin, S., & Potenza, M.N. (2012). The relationship between age of gambling onset and adolescent problematic gambling severity. *Journal of Psychiatric Research, 46*(5), 675–683.

Raylu, N. & Oei, T.P. (2004). Role of culture in gambling and problem gambling. *Clinical Psychology Review, 23*(8), 1087–1114.

Reilly, C. (2017). *Responsible gambling: A review of the research.* National Center for Responsible Gaming: White Paper.

Reuter, J., Raedler, T., Rose, M., Hand, I., Glasher, J. & Buchel, C. (2005). Pathological gambling is linked to reduced activation of the mesolimbic reward system. *Natural Neuroscience, 8*(2), 147–148.

Richard, J., Martin-Storey, A., Wilkie, E., Derevensky, J.L., Paskus, T., & Temcheff, C.E. (2019). Variations in gambling disorder symptomatology across sexual identity among college student-athletes. *Journal of Gambling Studies,* 1–14.

Rickwood, D., Blaszczynski, A., Delfabbro, P., Dowling, N., & Heading, K. (2010). The psychology of gambling. *InPsych, 32,* 11–21.

Rider, G.N., McMorris, B.J., Gower, A.L., Coleman, E., & Eisenberg, M.E. (2019). Gambling behaviors and problem gambling: A population-based comparison of transgender/gender diverse and cisgender adolescents. *Journal of Gambling Studies, 35*(1), 79–92.

Riley, B. (2014). Experiential avoidance mediates the association between thought suppression and mindfulness with problem gambling. *Journal of Gambling Studies, 30*, 163–171.

Rollnick, S. & Allison, J. (2004). Motivational Interviewing. In N. Heather & T. Stockwell (eds), *The Essential Handbook of Treatment and Prevention of Alcohol Problems*. New York, NY: John Wiley & Sons.

Rollnick, S. & Miller, W.R. (1995). What is motivational interviewing? *Behavioural and Cognitive Psychotherapy, 23*(4), 325–334.

Ronzitti, S., Kraus, S.W., Decker, S.E., & Ashrafioun, L. (2019). Clinical characteristics of veterans with gambling disorders seeking pain treatment. *Addictive Behaviors, 95*, 160–165.

Russell, A.M.T., Hing, N., Browne, M., Li, E., & Vitartas, P. (2019). Who bets on micro events (microbets) in sports? *Journal of Gambling Studies, 35*(1), 205.

SBIRT (n.d.). Accessed on 05/21/20 at www.integration.samhsa.gov/clinical-practice/sbirt.

Scherrer, J.F., Xian, H., Kapp, J.M.K., Waterman, B., Shah, K.R., Volberg, R., & Eisen, S.A. (2007). Association between exposure to childhood and lifetime traumatic events and lifetime pathological gambling in a twin cohort. *The Journal of Nervous and Mental Disease, 195*(1), 72–78.

Scholes-Balog, K.E. & Hemphill, S.A. (2012). Relationships between online gambling, mental health, and substance use: A review. *CyberPsychology, Behavior & Social Networking, 15*(12), 688–692.

Schwartz, D. (2013). *Roll the Bones: The History of Gambling, Casino Edition*. Las Vegas, NV: Winchester Books.

Segal, Z.V., Williams, J.M.G., & Teasdale, J. (2002). *Mindfulness-Based Cognitive Therapy for Depression: A New Approach to Preventing Relapse*. New York, NY: Guilford Press.

Shaffer, H.J. (1997). The most important unresolved issue in the addictions: Conceptual chaos. *Substance Use and Misuse, 32*(11), 1573–1580.

Shaffer, H.J. & Kidman, R. (eds). (2003). Shifting perspectives on gambling and addiction. *Journal of Gambling Studies, 19*, 1–6.

Shaffer, H.J., LaBrie, R., Scanlan, K.M, & Cummings, T.N. (1994). Pathological gambling among adolescents: Massachusetts gambling screen (MAGS). *Journal of Gambling Studies, 10*(4), 339–362.

Sharpe, L. (2002). A reformulated cognitive–behavioral model of problem gambling: A bio-psychosocial perspective. *Clinical Psychology Review, 22*(1), 1–25.

Sharpe, L. & Tarrier, N. (1993). Towards a cognitive-behavioural theory of problem gambling. *The British Journal of Psychiatry, 162*(3), 407–412.

Silverman, K., Kaminski, B.J., Higgins, S.T., & Brady, J.V. (2011). Behavior Analysis and Treatment of Drug Addiction. In W.W. Fisher, C.C. Piazza, & H.S. Roane (eds), *Handbook of Applied Behavior Analysis*. New York, NY: Guilford Press.

Single, E., Collins, D., Easton, B., Harwood, H., Lapsley, H, Kopp, P., & Wilson, E. (2003). *International Guidelines for Estimating the Costs of Substance Abuse* 2e. Geneva: World Health Organization.

Smart Recovery (2020). *Self-Management and Recovery Training*. Accessed on 05/21/20 at www.smartrecovery.org.

Snippe, L., Boffo, M., Stewart, S.H., Dom, G., & Wiers, R.W. (2019). Innovative Treatment Approaches in Gambling Disorder. In A. Heinz, N. Romanczuk-Seiferth & M.N. Potenza (eds), *Gambling Disorder*. New York, NY: Springer, Cham.

Spitzer, R.L., Kroenke, K., Williams, J.B.W., & Lowe, B. (2006). A brief measure for assessing Generalized Anxiety Disorder: The GAD-7. *Archives of Internal Medicine, 10*, 1092–1097.

St-Pierre, R.A., Walker, D.M., Derevensky, J., & Gupta, R. (2014). How availability and accessibility of gambling venues influence problem gambling: A review of the literature. *Gaming Law Review and Economics, 18*(2), 150–172.

Stewart, M.J., Davis MacNevin, P.L., Hodgins, D.C., Barrett, S.P., Swansburg, J., & Stewart, S.H. (2016). Motivation-matched approach to the treatment of problem gambling: A case series pilot study. *Journal of Gambling Issues, 33*, 124–147.

Stinchfield, R. (2002). Reliability, validity, and classification accuracy of the South Oaks Gambling Screen (SOGS). *Addictive Behaviors, 27*, 1–19.

Stinchfield, R. & Winters, K. (2001). Outcome of Minnesota's gambling treatment programs. *Journal of Gambling Studies, 17*, 217–245.

Stucki, S. & Rihs-Middel, M. (2007). Prevalence of adult problem and pathological gambling between 2000 and 2005: An update. *Journal of Gambling Studies, 23*(3), 245–257,

Substance Abuse and Mental Health Services Administration (SAMHSA) (2020). *Peer Support*. Bringing recovery supports to scale: Technical assistance center strategy. Accessed on 05/21/20 at www.samhsa.gov/sites/default/files/programs_campaigns/brss_tacs/peer-sup-port-2017.pdf.

Suckling, J. & Nestor, L.J. (2017). The neurobiology of addiction: The perspective from magnetic resonance imaging present and future. *Addiction (Abingdon, England), 112*(2), 360–369.

Suurvali, H., Cordingley, J., Hodgins, D.C., & Cunningham, J. (2009). Barriers to seeking help for gambling problems: A review of the empirical literature. *Journal of Gambling Studies, 25*(3), 407–424.

Terrell, D. (1994). A test of the gambler's fallacy: Evidence from pari-mutuel games. *Journal of Risk and Uncertainty, 8*(3), 309–317.

Theriot, J. & Azadfard, M. (2019). *Opioid Antagonists*. StatPearls Publishing. Accessed on 05/21/20 at www.ncbi.nlm.nih.gov/books/NBK537079.

Theule, J., Hurl, K.E., Cheung, K., Ward, M., & Henrikson, B. (2019). Exploring the relationships between problem gambling and ADHD: A meta-analysis. *Journal of Attention Disorders, 23*(12), 1427–1437.

Thomas, S.A., Piterman, L., & Jackson, A.C. (2008). Problem gambling: What do general practitioners need to know and do about it? *The Medical Journal of Australia, 189*(3), 135–136.

Tippmann-Peikert, M., Park, J.G., Boeve, B.F., Shepard, J.W., & Silber, M.H. (2007). Pathologic gambling in patients with restless legs syndrome treated with dopaminergic agonists. *Neurology, 68*(4), 301–303.

Toce-Gerstein, M., Gerstein, D.R., & Volberg, R.A. (2003). A hierarchy of gambling disorders in the community. *Addiction, 98*(12), 1661–1672.

Toneatto, T., Pillai, S., & Courtice, E.L. (2014). Mindfulness-enhanced cognitive behavior therapy for problem gambling: A controlled pilot study. *International Journal of Mental Health and Addiction, 12*(2), 197–205.

Toneatto, T., Vettese, L., & Nguyen, L. (2007). The role of mindfulness in cognitive-behavioural treatment of problem gambling. *Journal of Gambling Issues, 19*, 91–100.

United States (2004). *The Health Insurance Portability and Accountability Act (HIPAA)*. Washington, D.C.: US Dept. of Labor, Employee Benefits Security Administration.

Valleur, M., Codina, I., Vénisse, J. L., Romo, L., Magalon, D., *et al.* (2016). Towards a validation of the three pathways model of pathological gambling. *Journal of Gambling Studies*, *32*(2), 757–771.

Van den Brink, W. (2012). Evidence-based pharmacological treatment of substance use disorders and pathological gambling. *Current Drug Abuse Reviews*, *5*(1), 3–31.

Van der Maas, M., Mann, R.E., McCready, J., Matheson, F.I., Turner, N.E., Hamilton, H.A., Schrans, T., & Ialomiteanu, A. (2017). Problem gambling in a sample of older adult casino gamblers: Associations with gambling participation and motivations. *Journal of Geriatric Psychiatry and Neurology*, *30*(1), 3–10.

VanderWeele, T.J., Li, S., Tsai, A.C., & Kawachi, I. (2016) Association between religious service attendance and lower suicide rates among US women. *JAMA Psychiatry*, *73*(8), 845–851.

Verdejo-Garcia, A., Chong, T.T.-J., Stout, J.C., Yücel, M., & London, E.D. (2018). Stages of dysfunctional decision-making in addiction. *Pharmacology Biochemistry and Behavior*, *164*, 99–105.

Volberg, R.A., McNamara, L.M., & Carris, K.L. (2018). Risk factors for problem gambling in California: Demographics, comorbidities and gambling participation. *Journal of Gambling Studies, 34*, 361–377.

Walker, M.B. (1992). *The Psychology of Gambling*. New York, NY: Permagon Press.

Waluk, O.R., Youssef, G.J., & Dowling, N.A. (2016). The relationship between problem gambling and attention deficit hyperactivity disorder. *Journal of Gambling Studies*, *32*(2), 591–604.

Wardle, H., Moody, A., Griffiths, M.D., Orford, J., & Volberg, R. (2011). Defining the online gambler and patterns of behaviour integration: Evidence from the British Gambling Prevalence Survey. *International Gambling Studies*, *11*, 339–356.

Wareham, J.D. & Potenza, M.N. (2010). Pathological gambling and substance use disorders. *The American Journal of Drug and Alcohol Abuse*, *36*(5), 242–247.

Weintraub, D., Koester, J., Potenza, M.N., Siderowf, A.D., *et al.* (2010). Impulse control disorders in Parkinson disease: A cross-sectional study of 3090 patients. *Archives of Neurology*, *67*(5), 589–595.

Welte, J., Barnes, G.M., Wieczorek, W., Tidwell, M.C., & Parker, J. (2001). Alcohol and gambling pathology among U.S. adults: Prevalence, demographic patterns and comorbidity. *Journal of Studies on Alcohol*, *62*(5). 706–712.

Welte, J.W., Wieczorek, W.F., Barnes, G.M., & Tidwell, M.C. (2006). Multiple risk factors for frequent and problem gambling: Individual, social, and ecological. *Journal of Applied Social Psychology*, *36*(6), 1548–1568.

Welte, J.W., Wieczorek, W.F., Barnes, G.M., Tidwell, M.C.O., & Hoffman, J.H. (2004). The relationship of ecological and geographic factors to gambling behavior and pathology. *Journal of Gambling Studies, 20*, 405–423.

West, B. (2008). *Strategic contingency management to enhance treatment outcomes for problem gamblers* [Master's Thesis]. University of Lethbridge, School of Health Sciences.

West, R. & Brown, J. (2013). *Theory of Addiction*. New York, NY: John Wiley & Sons.

Westphal, J.R. (2008). How well are we helping problem gamblers? An update to the evidence base supporting problem gambling treatment. *International Journal of Mental Health and Addiction*, *6*, 249–264.

Whiting, S.W. & Dixon, M.R. (2013). Effects of mental imagery on gambling behavior. *Journal of Gambling Studies, 29*, 525–534.

Wiebe, J. (2000). Prevalence of gambling and problem gambling among older adults in Manitoba. Addictions Foundation of Manitoba.

Wilber, M.K. & Potenza, M.N. (2006). Adolescent gambling: Research and clinical implications. *Psychiatry (Edgmont)*, 3(10), 40.

Williams, R.J., Volberg, R.A., & Stevens, R.M. (2012). *The population prevalence of problem gambling: Methodological influences, standardized rates, jurisdictional differences, and worldwide trends.* Ontario Problem Gambling Research Centre.

Williams, R.J., West, B.L., & Simpson, R.I. (2012). *Prevention of problem gambling: A comprehensive review of the evidence and identified best practices.* Ontario Problem Gambling Research Centre and the Ontario Ministry of Health and Long Term Care.

Wilson, A.N. & Matthieu, M. (2015). Applied Clinical Utility of Behavior Analysis and Social Work. In J. Ringdahl, T. Falcomata, & H. Roane (eds), *Clinical and Organizational Applications of Applied Behavior Analysis.* Amsterdam: Elsevier, Inc.

Wilson, A.N., Salas-Wright, C.P., Vaughn, M.G., & Maynard, B.R. (2015). Gambling prevalence rates among immigrants: A multigenerational examination. *Addictive Behaviors, 42*, 79–85.

Winters, K.C. & Derevensky, J.L. (2019). A review of sports wagering: Prevalence, characteristics of sports bettors, and association with problem gambling. *Journal of Gambling Issues, 43*, 102–127.

Witkiewitz, K., Bowen, S., Harrop, E.N., Douglas, H., Enkema, M., & Sedgwick, C. (2014). Mindfulness-based treatment to prevent addictive behavior relapse: Theoretical models and hypothesized mechanisms of change. *Substance Use & Misuse, 49*(5), 513–524.

Wohl, M.J., Gainsbury, S., Stewart, M.J., & Sztainert, T. (2013). Facilitating responsible gambling: The relative effectiveness of education-based animation and monetary limit setting pop-up messages among electronic gaming machine players. *Journal of Gambling Studies, 29*(4), 703–717.

Wohl, M.J. & Sztainert, T. (2011). Where did all the pathological gamblers go? Gambling symptomatology and stage of change predict attrition in longitudinal research. *Journal of Gambling Studies, 27*(1), 155–169.

Wood, R.T.A., Gupta, R., Derevensky, J.L., & Griffiths, M. (2004). Video game playing and gambling in adolescents: Common risk factors. *Journal of Child & Adolescent Substance Abuse, 14*(1), 77–100.

Wood, R.T. & Williams, R.J., (2011). A comparative profile of the Internet gambler: Demographic characteristics, game-play patterns, and problem gambling status. *New Media & Society. 13*, 1123–1141.

Wood, R.T., Williams, R.J., & Lawton, P.K. (2007). Why do Internet gamblers prefer online versus land-based venues? Some preliminary findings and implications. *Journal of Gambling Issues. 20*, 235–252.

World Health Organization (2019). *International Statistical Classification of Diseases and Related Health Problems (11th ed.).* Accessed on 05/21/20 at https://icd.who.int.

World Health Organization. (2018). *International Classification of Diseases for Mortality and Morbidity Statistics* (11th Revision). Accessed on 05/21/20 at https://icd.who.int/browse11/l-m/en.

Yakovenko, I., Quigley, L., Hemmelgarn, B.R., Hodgins, D.C., & Ronksley, P. (2015). The efficacy of motivational interviewing for disordered gambling: Systematic review and meta-analysis. *Addictive Behaviors, 43*, 72–82.

Yau, Y.H.C., Crowley, M.J., Mayes, L.C., & Potenza, M.N. (2012). Are Internet use and video-game-playing addictive behaviors? Biological, clinical and public health implications for youths and adults. *Minerva Psichiatrica, 53*(3), 153.

Subject Index

Author Index